SESAME STREET PARENTS

Christmas

Holiday Projects for Parents & Children

Edited by
Shannon Sexton Jernigan

Oxmoor House®

Sesame Street Parents Christmas

©1998 Children's Television Workshop and Oxmoor House, Inc. Jim Henson's Sesame Street Muppet Characters ©1998 The Jim Henson Company. Sesame Street and the Sesame Street Sign are trademarks and service marks of Children's Television Workshop. A portion of the money you pay for this book goes to Children's Television Workshop. It is put right back into SESAME STREET and other CTW educational projects. Thanks for helping!

Please visit our website at www.sesamestreet.com

Sesame Street Parents is a trademark of Children's Television Workshop.
Oxmoor House, Inc.
Book Division of Southern Progress Corporation
P.O. Box 2463, Birmingham, AL 35201

Library of Congress Catalog Card Number: 98-067022
Hardcover ISBN: 0-8487-1823-2
Softcover ISBN: 0-8487-1841-0
ISSN: 1099-8055
Manufactured in the United States of America
First Printing 1998

We're here for you!
We at Oxmoor House are dedicated to serving you with reliable information that expands your imagination and enriches your life. We welcome your comments and suggestions. Please write us at:

    Oxmoor House, Inc.
    Editor, *Sesame Street Parents Christmas*
    2100 Lakeshore Drive
    Birmingham, AL 35209
To order additional publications, call 1-205-877-6560.

Oxmoor House, Inc.
Editor-in-Chief: Nancy Fitzpatrick Wyatt
Senior Homes Editor: Mary Kay Culpepper
Senior Foods Editor: Susan Payne Stabler
Senior Editor, Editorial Services: Olivia Kindig Wells
Art Director: James Boone

Sesame Street Parents Christmas
Editor: Shannon Sexton Jernigan
Designer: Teresa Kent
Copy Editors: Donna Baldone, L. Amanda Owens
Photo Stylist: Connie Formby
Illustrators: Barbara Ball, Kelly Davis, Emily Albright Parrish
Contributing Editors: Catherine Corbett Fowler,
        Linda Martin Stewart, Linda Baltzell Wright
Senior Photographer: John O'Hagan
Director, Production and Distribution: Phillip Lee
Associate Production Manager: Vanessa Cobbs Richardson
Production Assistant: Faye Porter Bonner

Put Safety First

The activities in this book are designed to be used by an adult and a child working together. Please be sure to follow appropriate safety precautions, especially when using scissors or when cooking in the kitchen with your child. When using art materials, such as paint, glue, or small beads, make sure that young children do not put anything in their mouths. Be especially careful with all small items that may cause a child to choke.

Dear Parents,

The wonder of the Christmas season is reflected in the imaginations of children. In **Sesame Street Parents Christmas,** you'll find ideas that will spark your children's creativity while giving you the chance to spend meaningful time together during the holiday season.

In "Reindeer Games" and "Merry Munchies," your children will discover games, party favors, and kid-tested refreshments. They'll trim your home with handmade treasures found in "Holiday House," which features projects like garlands, stockings, and wreaths. In "Presents to Make" you'll be delighted to find inexpensive gift ideas they can make for teachers and friends, such as **Surprise Balls** and **Dip-and-Drip Flowerpots.** Let your kids browse through "Grin and Wear It" for wearables like **Merry Mittens, Reindeer Hats,** and **Button-Tree Tops.** Whatever your child's skill level, the projects in this book offer something just right.

Now, let the crafting begin! And enjoy watching little hands make some big holiday fun.

The Editors

Contents

wands, page 36
aprons, page 134

ornaments, page 46

pots, page 74

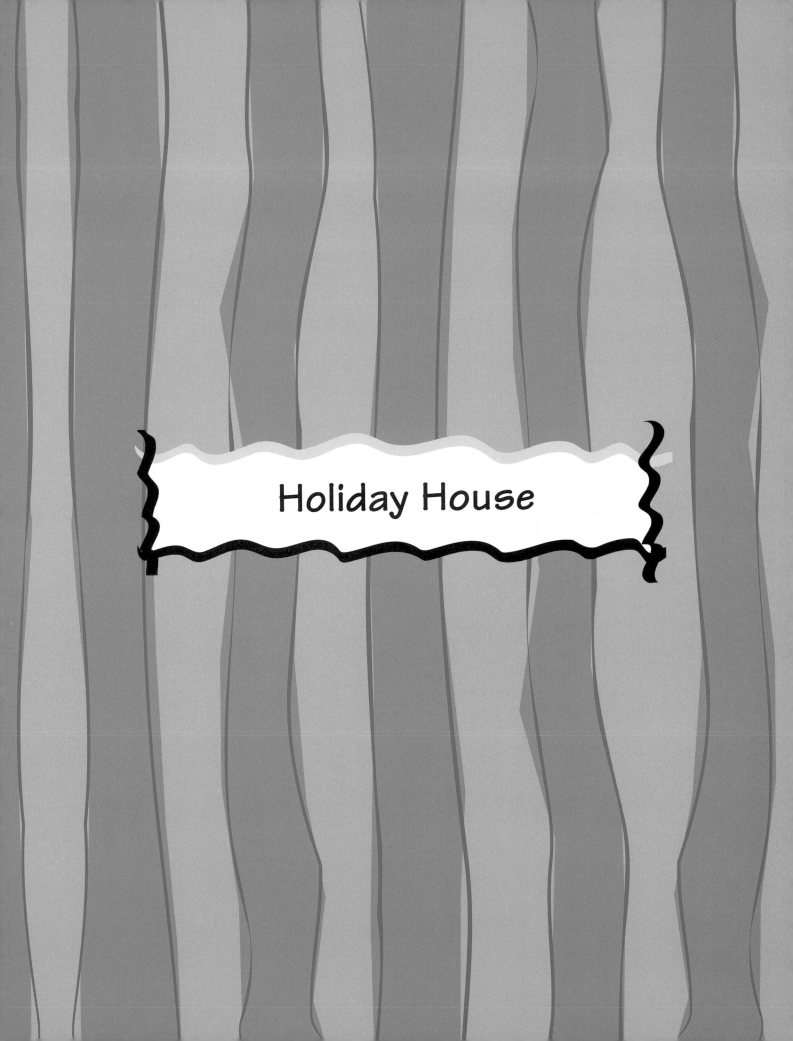

Holiday House

Miniature Stockings

You will need (for each stocking):

- Patterns on page 10
- Tracing paper
- Sharp pencil
- Scissors
- ¼ yard felt
- Colored felt scraps
- Hole punch
- Large-eyed needle
- 40" length yarn
- Glue

Big Bird hangs little felt stockings by the chimney with care. They are so quick and cute, your kids can make some to share.

1. Trace the patterns and the markings. Cut out.

8

2. From the felt, cut 2 stockings. Be sure to mark the holes for stitching. Cut the decorations from the felt scraps.

3. With the hole punch, make the hole for the hanger in the circle at the top of the stocking. Punch out the rest of the holes with the point of the pencil.

4. Thread the needle with the yarn. Knot 1 end of the yarn. Place 1 stocking on top of the other and hold them together. Start sewing on the side opposite the hanger circle. Sew through the holes all around the edges of the stocking. Then slide the needle off the yarn and make a loop through the large hole for the hanger. Tie the end of the yarn to the last stitch on the back of the stocking. Clip the end.

5. To decorate the stocking, glue the different-colored shapes to the stocking front.

Stocking
Cut 2.

10

Holly-Leaf Wreath

Happy holly-days! For a fun group project, children can cut out the leaves, glue them together in a circle and add a bow.

1. Trace the pan onto 1 sheet of green paper. Cut out the circle.

2. Place the salad plate in the center of the circle. Draw around the plate. Cut out the small circle to make a wreath form.

3. Trace and cut out the holly leaf. Fold a sheet of green paper in half and trace the leaf onto the paper as many times as possible. Repeat as needed to trace 18 leaves. Cut out the leaves and unfold them.

4. Glue the leaves around the wreath form. Use the paper clips to hold the leaves in place until the glue dries.

5. Using the ribbon, tie a bow. Pull the wire through the back of the bow knot. Poke 2 holes in the wreath and pull the ends of the wire through the holes. Twist the ends together.

You will need:
- Pattern below
- Pencil
- Round pan (about 13" across)
- Several sheets heavy-weight green paper
- Scissors
- Salad plate (about 8" across)
- Tracing paper
- Craft glue
- Paper clips
- Ribbon for bow
- Thin wire

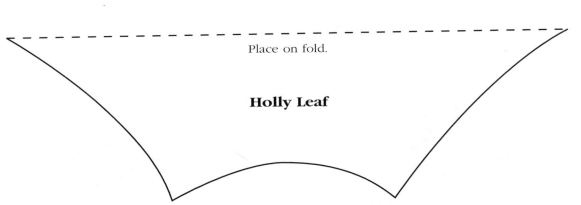

Place on fold.

Holly Leaf

11

Star Garland

Gumdrop Garland

Great Garlands

Elmo adds sparkle to his tree with a string of stars, and your kids can, too. All you need are drinking straws and paper or candy.

Note: For longer garlands, tie the 4' garland lengths together.

Star

Star Garland

1. Trace the star pattern. Cut out. Transfer the pattern to the posterboard and the corrugated paper. Cut out the stars.

2. Cut the drinking straws into 2" lengths.

You will need (for 1 star garland):

- Pattern above
- Pencil
- Tracing paper
- Scissors
- Yellow poster-board
- Yellow corru-gated paper
- Colored plastic drinking straws
- Tapestry needle
- String

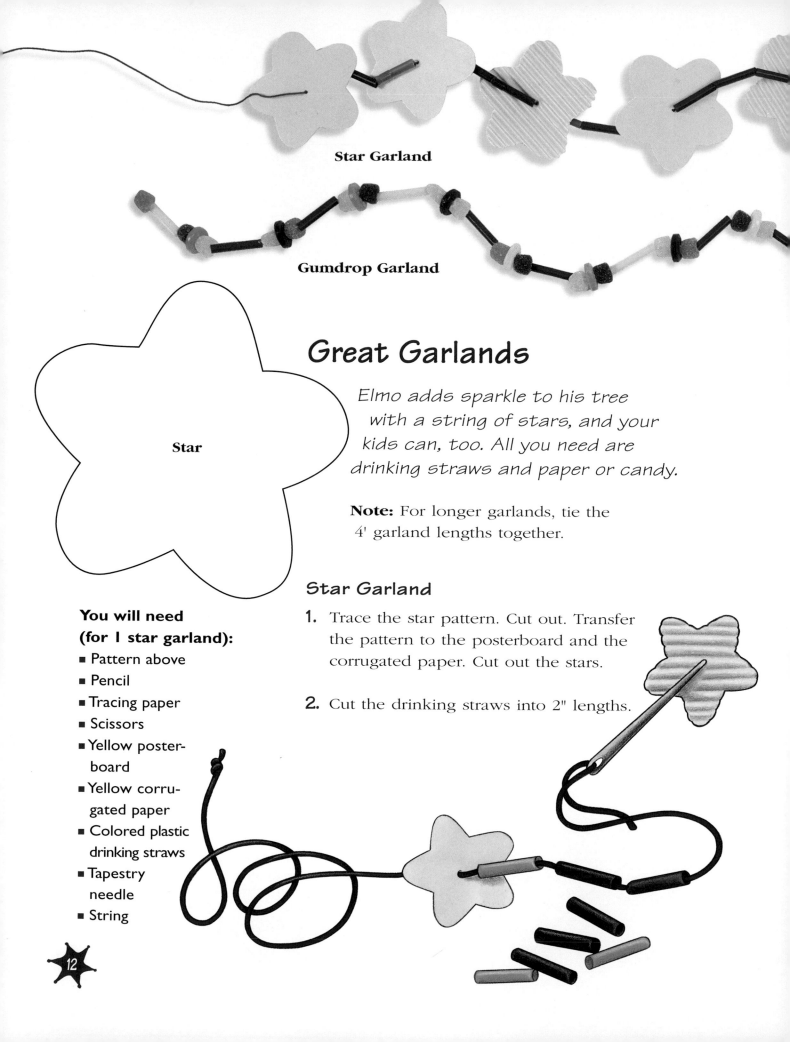

3. Thread the needle with a 4' piece of string. Tie a big knot at 1 end. With the needle, poke a hole in the center of a star and run the needle and the string through it. Run the needle and the string through 3 pieces of straw. Then run the needle and the string through another star and 3 more straw pieces. Keep doing this until you reach 6" from the end of the string. Slide the needle off and tie a big knot in the end of the string.

Gumdrop Garland

1. Cut the drinking straws into 2" lengths.

2. Thread the tapestry needle with a 4' piece of string. Tie a big knot at 1 end. Run the threaded needle through a gumdrop, a ring candy, a gumdrop, and a piece of straw. Keep doing this until you reach 6" from the end of the string. Slide the needle off and tie a big knot in the end of the string.

You will need (for 1 gumdrop garland):
- Colored plastic drinking straws
- Scissors
- Tapestry needle
- String
- Gumdrops
- Fruit-flavored ring candies

Terrific Tree Skirt

Bert and Ernie decorated some felt rectangles with ribbons and then glued them to a green felt circle. They'll always find these "packages" under their Christmas tree—even if Santa hasn't visited yet.

You will need:

- Pencil or marker
- 36" length string
- Pushpin
- 2 yards 72"-wide green felt
- Scissors
- Fabric glue
- Liquid ravel preventer
- Variety of ribbons
- Ruler
- 7½ yards giant white rickrack
- Felt rectangles: 8 colors (For white and yellow, use double layers so that the green felt won't show through.)
- Twist ties

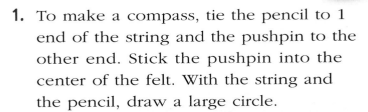

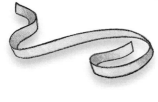

1. To make a compass, tie the pencil to 1 end of the string and the pushpin to the other end. Stick the pushpin into the center of the felt. With the string and the pencil, draw a large circle.

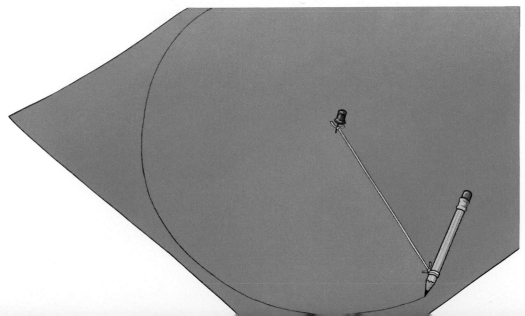

2. Cut the string to 5" and make a small circle in the center of the large circle. Cut out the large circle. Cut straight up from the edge of the large circle to the small circle and then cut out the small circle to make an opening for the tree trunk.

3. With fabric glue, glue the rickrack to the inner and outer edges of the circle. Apply liquid ravel preventer to the ends of the rickrack to keep the ends from fraying.

4. To make the packages, choose ribbons to coordinate with each felt rectangle. Measure across the width, down the length, or diagonally across a felt piece. Cut the ribbon to that length.

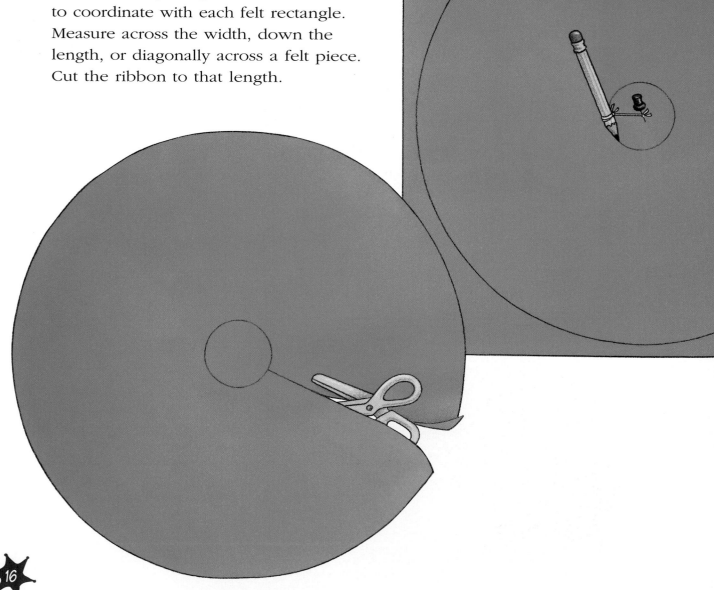

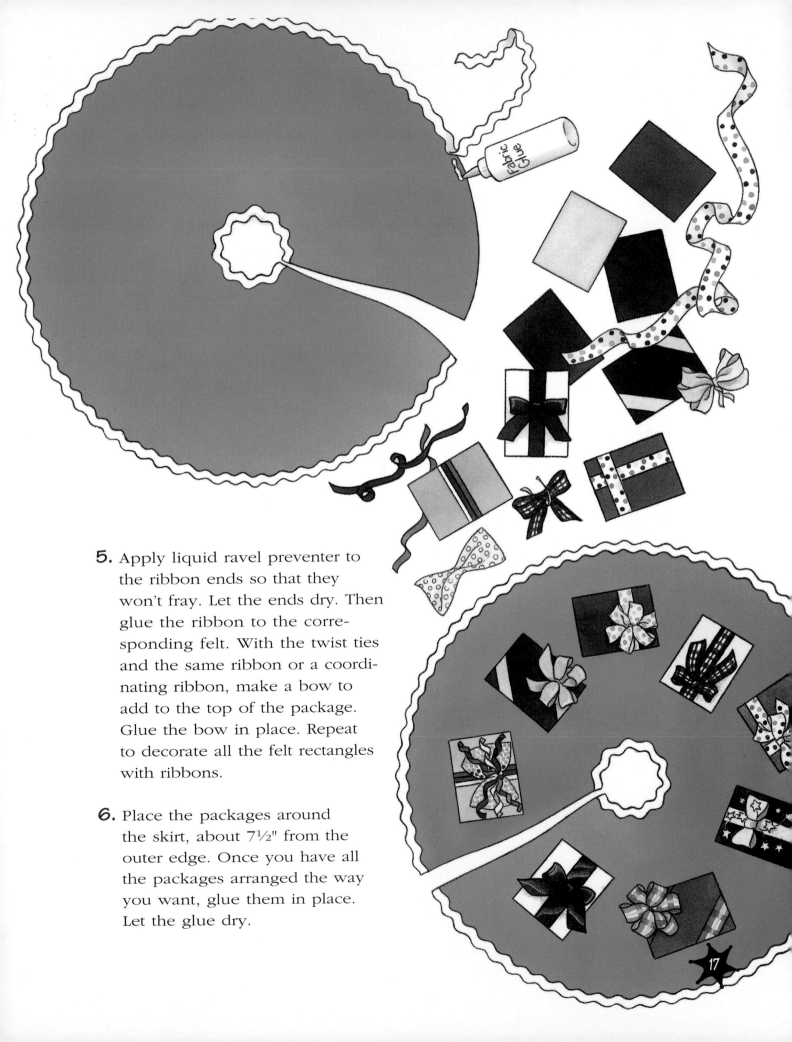

5. Apply liquid ravel preventer to the ribbon ends so that they won't fray. Let the ends dry. Then glue the ribbon to the corresponding felt. With the twist ties and the same ribbon or a coordinating ribbon, make a bow to add to the top of the package. Glue the bow in place. Repeat to decorate all the felt rectangles with ribbons.

6. Place the packages around the skirt, about 7½" from the outer edge. Once you have all the packages arranged the way you want, glue them in place. Let the glue dry.

17

You will need:

- 8½" x 11" sheets green paper
- Pencils
- Scissors
- Paper and tape for covering door
- Glue stick
- Paper for cutouts

Handy-dandy Door Decoration

Here's a super idea for your child's class-room or bedroom door.

1. Give a sheet of green paper to each person.

2. Ask each person to draw around his or her hand on the paper as shown and cut it out.

3. Cover the door with the door paper.

4. Fold each hand about 2" from the straight edge. Starting at the bottom and working toward the top, glue each hand along the folded edge to the door to make a tree shape.

5. Using the photograph for inspiration, decorate the tree and the door with paper cutouts.

19

Magical Magnets

Stick 'em up! Grover uses these colorful magnets to hang artwork on the refrigerator.

1. Trace and cut out the desired patterns.

2. Transfer the patterns to the tray and cut them out.

3. Paint the shapes, letting the paint dry between colors. Add the details, using a small paintbrush. Let the paint dry.

4. Outline each shape with the squeeze paint. Let the paint dry completely.

5. For each, cut a piece of magnetic tape and glue it to the back of the shape.

You will need:
- Patterns on pages 22–23
- Pencil
- Tracing paper
- Scissors
- White foam trays (clean and dry)
- Acrylic paints in assorted colors
- Paintbrushes in assorted sizes
- White acrylic paint in squeeze tube
- Roll of magnetic strip tape
- White glue

Angel

Gingerbread Man

Star

Present

22

Stocking

Candy Cane

Snowman

Tree

23

Fun Foam Forest

Little legs don't need a ladder to trim these trees! And children can make all the decorations themselves.

1. Choose the desired size tree—small, medium, or large. Trace and cut out the desired tree and star patterns. Trace the patterns 2 times onto the color foam indicated. Cut them out, making sure to mark the bottom center of each triangle.

2. To make the star, glue the pieces together along the outside edges, leaving the bottom unglued. Set the star aside.

3. Using the water-soluble marker and the ruler, draw a straight line from the peak of the tree to the bottom center on 1 side of each triangle. Mark the center point of the tree on each line. On 1 triangle, cut along the marked line from the peak to the center point. On the other triangle, cut along the marked line from the bottom to the center point.

You will need (for each tree):
- Patterns on pages 26–27
- Tracing paper
- Pencil
- Scissors
- Fun Foam: green, yellow, blue, black, red, orange, white
- Founder's Adhesive glue
- Water-soluble marker
- Ruler
- Hole punch (optional)

For the teardrop-lights tree:
- Fine-point permanent black marker

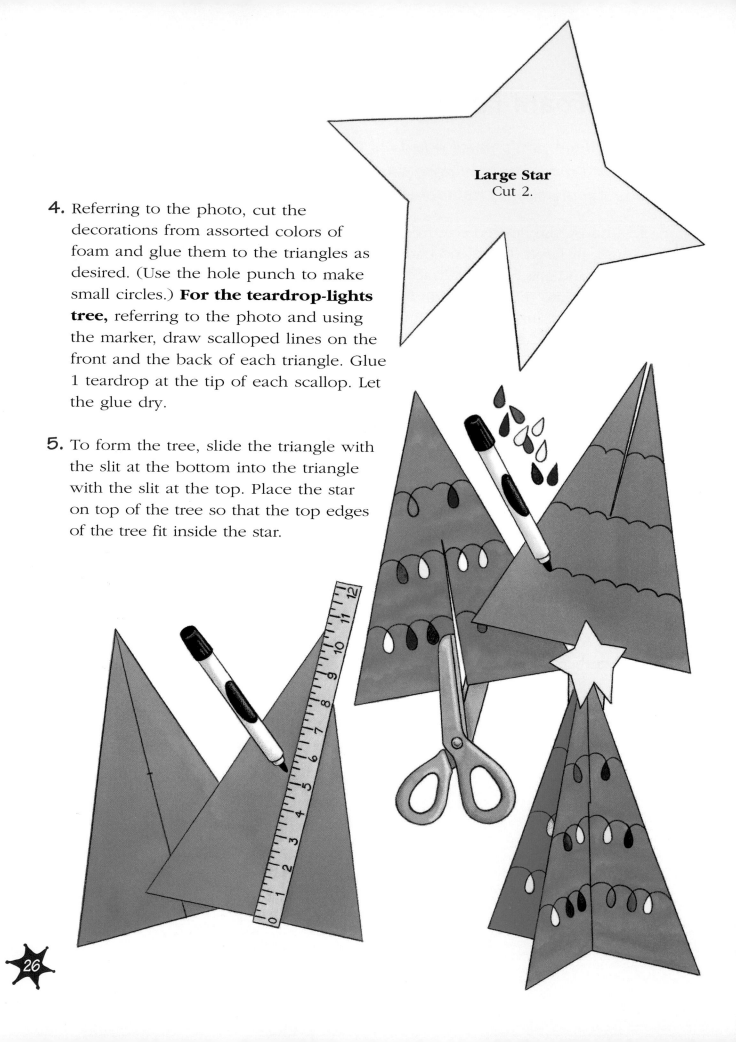

Large Star
Cut 2.

4. Referring to the photo, cut the decorations from assorted colors of foam and glue them to the triangles as desired. (Use the hole punch to make small circles.) **For the teardrop-lights tree,** referring to the photo and using the marker, draw scalloped lines on the front and the back of each triangle. Glue 1 teardrop at the tip of each scallop. Let the glue dry.

5. To form the tree, slide the triangle with the slit at the bottom into the triangle with the slit at the top. Place the star on top of the tree so that the top edges of the tree fit inside the star.

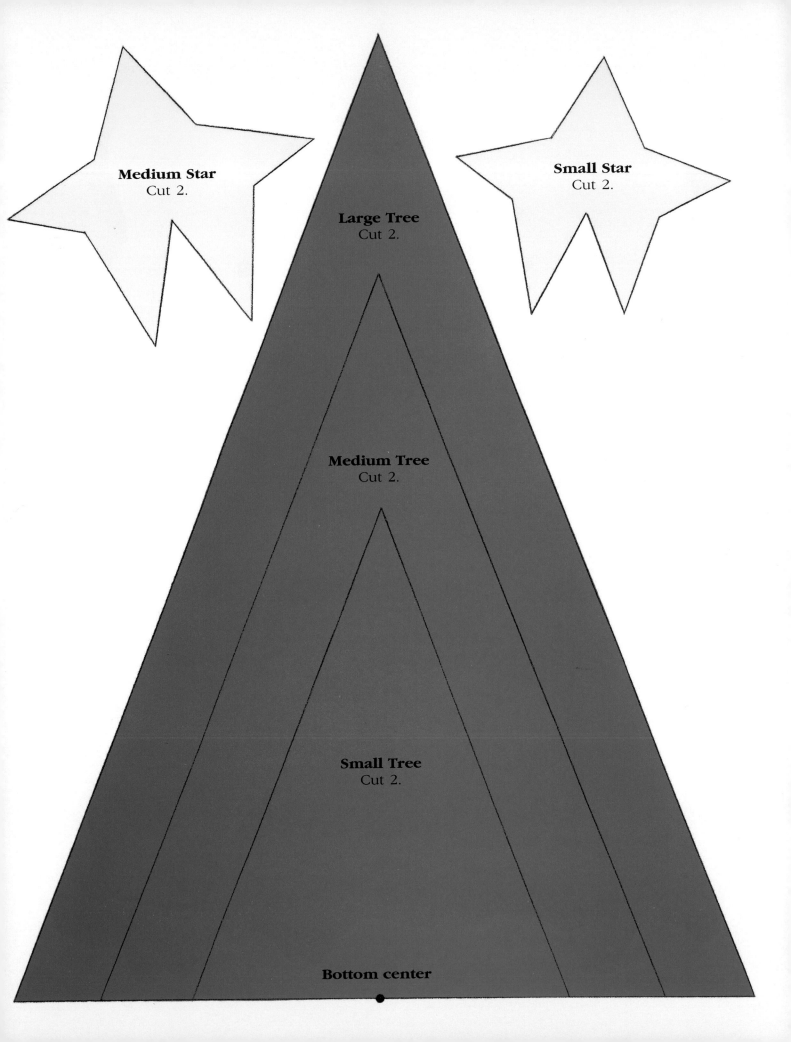

Medium Star
Cut 2.

Small Star
Cut 2.

Large Tree
Cut 2.

Medium Tree
Cut 2.

Small Tree
Cut 2.

Bottom center

Merry Munchies

Chocolate-Covered Snowballs

Join in the fun with a child when you dip marshmallows into chocolate for a chewy snack.

**You will need
(for 5 dozen):**
- Waxed paper
- 1 (8-ounce) package chocolate almond bark
- Microwave-safe bowl
- Large wooden spoon
- 1 (1-pound) package large marshmallows
- Plastic straws in assorted colors
- Multicolored nonpareils

1. Cover your work surface with the waxed paper. Break the almond bark into small pieces and place them in the bowl. Following the manufacturer's instructions, melt the almond bark. Stir until smooth.

2. Spear 1 marshmallow with a plastic straw. Dip it into the almond bark mixture, letting the excess drip back into the bowl. Sprinkle nonpareils onto the marshmallow and then place it on the waxed paper to dry. Repeat for the other snowballs.

Campfire Cocoa

Ernie mixes up this chocolaty drink in a flash. Then he stirs in extra flavor and fun with marshmallows and candy-cane sticks.

1. Combine the first 4 ingredients in the bowl. Secure the lid. Shake well to mix.

2. To serve, combine ½ cup of mix and 1 cup of hot water in a mug. Stir with a candy cane and top with marshmallows.

3. For each package, pour the desired amount of mix into the jar and screw on the lid. Wrap the candy canes in the clear cellophane and the marshmallows in the red cellophane. Tie each end with a piece of curling ribbon and then tie both packages on top of the jar. Fold the card stock in half and punch a hole in the center top. Label the mix on the card front and write the serving instructions on the inside. Tie the card to the jar with curling ribbon.

You will need (for 10 cups):
- 2 cups chocolate powdered drink mix
- 2½ cups powdered sugar
- 1 (11-ounce) jar powdered creamer
- 12 cups dry powdered milk
- Large bowl with lid

For each package:
- Small clear jar with lid
- 6 old-fashioned candy canes
- ¾ cup miniature marshmallows
- 1 sheet each clear and red cellophane
- ⅝ yard red curling ribbon
- 3" x 6" piece card stock
- Hole punch
- Red marker

31

Bubble-Gum Baubles

Kids can string gum balls on dental floss to make colorful necklaces like Zoe's. Best of all, when they're finished wearing them, they make a tasty treat.

**You will need
(for I necklace and
I bracelet):**

- Ice pick
- 20 to 26 candy-coated gum balls
- 42" length dental floss
- Large-eyed needle

1. Pierce a hole all the way through each gum ball with the ice pick. (**Note:** Child will need help with this step.)

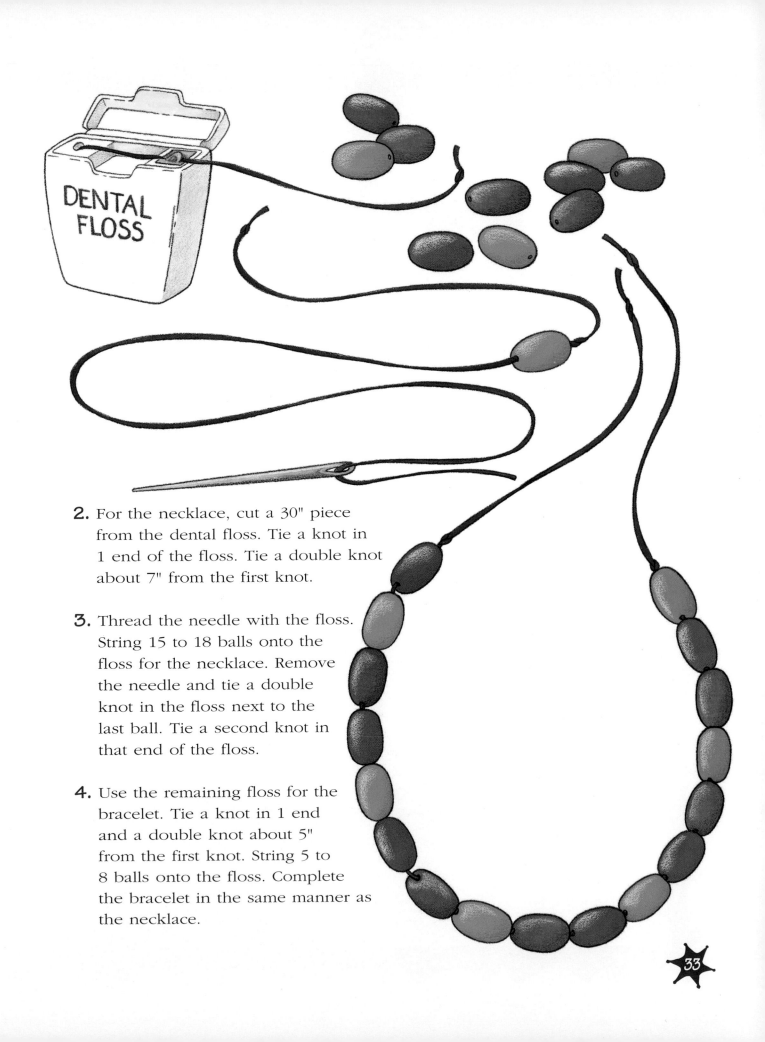

2. For the necklace, cut a 30" piece from the dental floss. Tie a knot in 1 end of the floss. Tie a double knot about 7" from the first knot.

3. Thread the needle with the floss. String 15 to 18 balls onto the floss for the necklace. Remove the needle and tie a double knot in the floss next to the last ball. Tie a second knot in that end of the floss.

4. Use the remaining floss for the bracelet. Tie a knot in 1 end and a double knot about 5" from the first knot. String 5 to 8 balls onto the floss. Complete the bracelet in the same manner as the necklace.

33

Candy-Cane Mice

"Me like candy canes," Cookie Monster says. So on the night before Christmas, Cookie hangs on the tree green felt mice just as cute as can be!

1. Trace and transfer the patterns and the markings. Cut out.

2. From the green felt, cut 1 body and 2 ears. From the red felt, cut 2 inner ears. Cut slits in the body where marked on the pattern.

3. Center and glue 1 inner ear on 1 ear. Repeat for the other ear. Glue the wiggle eyes and the pom-pom nose to the body. Let the glue dry.

4. With the red side up, slide the thin end of 1 ear through 1 ear slit. Repeat with the other ear. Turn the mouse over and glue the end of each ear to the back of the mouse. Let the glue dry. Slide a candy cane through the candy cane slits on the body.

You will need (for I mouse):
- Patterns below
- Tracing paper
- Pencil
- Scissors
- Felt: green, red
- Fabric glue
- Wiggle eyes
- Red pom-pom
- Candy cane

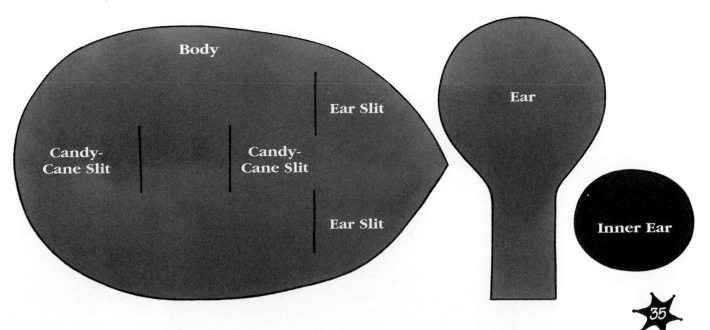

Body

Ear Slit

Candy-Cane Slit

Candy-Cane Slit

Ear Slit

Ear

Inner Ear

35

You will need
(for 4 wands):

- Pattern at right
- 1 (1-pound) box instant dissolving sugar
- 1 (4-ounce) container red sugar crystals
- ½ (7.5-ounce) container orange-flavored breakfast beverage mix
- 1 (.13-ounce) package cherry-flavored unsweetened soft-drink mix
- Large mixing bowl
- Large wooden spoon
- Zip-top plastic bag
- Tracing paper
- Pencil
- Scissors
- Posterboard
- Dot stickers in assorted sizes
- 4 (9" x 36") pieces netting
- 4 pipe cleaners
- Tacky glue
- 4 (12") pieces clear plastic tubing
- ½"-wide red plastic tape
- 8 corks to fit the ends of the tubes
- Funnel

Stardust Wands

A sweet-and-sour powdered treat is fun to eat straight from a Stardust Wand. Follow the secret recipe to make four wands—there will be some stardust left over for Grover, too.

1. To make about 3 cups of stardust, combine the first 4 ingredients in the bowl. Stir them together until everything is well blended. Store the mixture in the zip-top bag until you're ready to fill the tubes.

Star

2. Trace the star pattern and cut it out. From the posterboard, cut 1 star for each wand. Decorate each star with stickers.

3. Gather 1 piece of netting. To make a bow, wrap a pipe cleaner around the middle of the netting, leaving the ends free. Glue a star to the netting, covering the pipe cleaner. Repeat to make 3 more bows.

4. Starting at 1 end, wrap 1 tube with the red tape to resemble a candy cane. Repeat with the other 3 tubes.

5. Push a cork in 1 end of the tube so that it fits very tightly. Place the funnel in the opposite end. While you hold the funnel, have a friend pour the stardust into the funnel to fill the tube. When the tube is full, push a cork in the open end. Place a dot sticker on the end of each cork. Repeat to fill the remaining 3 tubes.

6. To add the bow, twist the ends of the pipe cleaner around 1 end of the tube. Repeat to decorate the remaining tubes in the same manner.

You will need:

- 1 (½-ounce) chewy fruit roll
- Ruler
- Kitchen shears
- 1 small tube cake-decorating writing gel
- Plastic wrap
- 1 (6-ounce) package bite-sized fish-shaped crackers
- 1 (10-ounce) box bite-sized round snack crackers

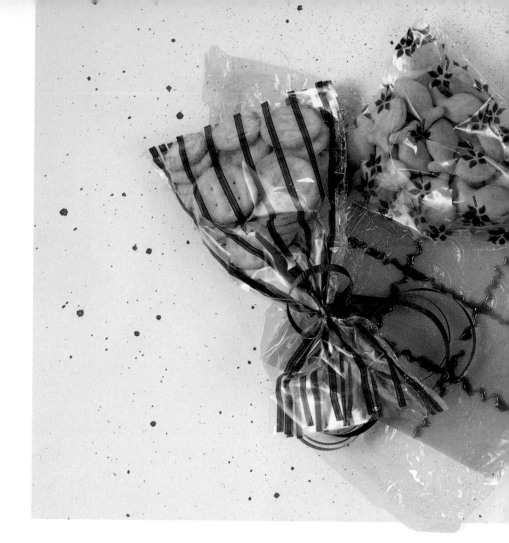

Eat 'Em Up Tic-tac-toe

The winner of this game gets to eat all of the game pieces! That's why Bert likes to make these tic-tac-toe sets for gifts. Each set has one gameboard and two different kinds of crackers for markers.

1. Unroll the fruit roll and press it flat. Remove the cellophane and throw it away. Using the kitchen shears, cut the roll into a 4½" x 3½" rectangle.

2. Using even pressure, lightly squeeze the gel and draw a tic-tac-toe grid on the fruit roll as shown.

3. Lightly cover the rectangle with plastic wrap and let it stand overnight at room temperature.

4. Use the fish-shaped crackers as 1 set of game pieces and the round crackers as the other set.

Reindeer Games

Santa-Sack Relay

Grover and Big Bird cheer on the contestants in a jumping Christmas race. To participate, kids piece together strips of fabric like a puzzle and glue them to a laundry bag. The instructions even include the rules of the game.

You will need
(for 2 sacks):

- Patterns below
- Tracing paper
- Pencil
- Scissors
- Yardstick
- ⅓ yard yellow felt
- 45"-wide cotton fabric: ⅞ yard black, ⅝ yard red
- ⅓ yard 45"-wide white polyester fleece
- Liquid ravel preventer
- 2 (28" x 36") white laundry bags
- Fabric glue

1. Trace and cut out the belt buckle and boot buckle patterns. Transfer each pattern to the felt as indicated and cut them out. Set the buckles aside.

2. From the black fabric, cut 2 (5" x 28") strips and 2 (12" x 24") rectangles. From the red fabric, cut 2 (7" x 28") strips and 4 (6" x 7") strips. From the fleece, cut 2 (5" x 28") strips.

3. To make the boots, measure and mark each black rectangle as shown at right. Then cut along the broken lines to make 2 boots from each rectangle.

4. Apply liquid ravel preventer to the cut edges of all the black and red pieces.

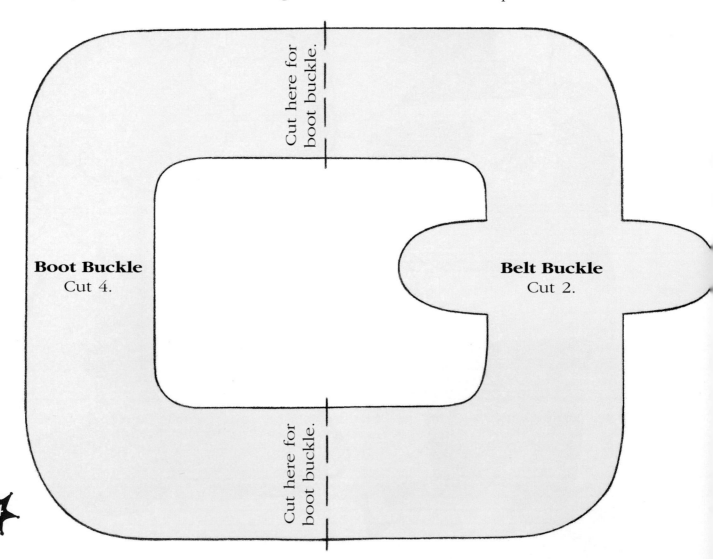

Cut here for boot buckle.

Cut here for boot buckle.

Boot Buckle
Cut 4.

Belt Buckle
Cut 2.

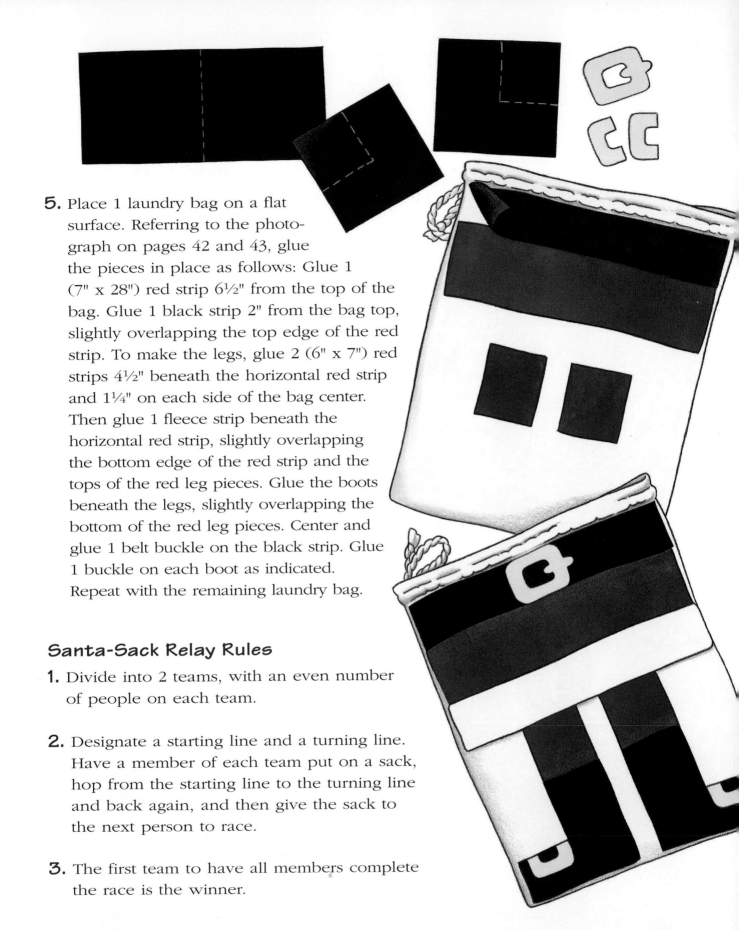

5. Place 1 laundry bag on a flat surface. Referring to the photograph on pages 42 and 43, glue the pieces in place as follows: Glue 1 (7" x 28") red strip 6½" from the top of the bag. Glue 1 black strip 2" from the bag top, slightly overlapping the top edge of the red strip. To make the legs, glue 2 (6" x 7") red strips 4½" beneath the horizontal red strip and 1¼" on each side of the bag center. Then glue 1 fleece strip beneath the horizontal red strip, slightly overlapping the bottom edge of the red strip and the tops of the red leg pieces. Glue the boots beneath the legs, slightly overlapping the bottom of the red leg pieces. Center and glue 1 belt buckle on the black strip. Glue 1 buckle on each boot as indicated. Repeat with the remaining laundry bag.

Santa-Sack Relay Rules

1. Divide into 2 teams, with an even number of people on each team.

2. Designate a starting line and a turning line. Have a member of each team put on a sack, hop from the starting line to the turning line and back again, and then give the sack to the next person to race.

3. The first team to have all members complete the race is the winner.

Go Fish!

Kids can make a dozen of these fun fish and join Elmo for a game of Go Fish. When the game is over, the players can take home their catch to hang on the Christmas tree.

1. Trace and cut out the patterns. Transfer the patterns to the foam as indicated and cut them out.

2. For each fish, use the paint pens to draw stripes on 1 side of the side fins and on both sides of the top fins and the tails as indicated. Set them aside.

3. Position the ornament so that the hanger attachment is to 1 side. Using a paint pen, start at the center top and draw 3 V shapes on each side. Color in the design with the paint pen. Let the paint dry.

4. Glue 1 wiggle eye on each side of the ornament near the hanger attachment (see the photograph).

5. Glue 2 side fins, 1 top fin, and 1 tail to the ornament as shown. Let the glue dry. Repeat for the remaining fish.

You will need (for 12 fish):
- Patterns on page 49
- Tracing paper
- Pencil
- Scissors
- Fun Foam in assorted colors
- Paint pens in assorted colors
- 12 plastic ball ornaments in assorted colors
- Founder's Adhesive glue
- 24 (15-mm) wiggle eyes

**You will need
(for 2 fishing poles):**

- Waxed paper
- 2 (36"-long) ⅜"-
  diameter wooden
  dowels
- Yellow spray paint
- Pencil
- Ruler
- 3¾ yards ¼"-wide red
  grosgrain ribbon, cut in
  half
- Scissors
- Founder's Adhesive glue
- 2 (18" x 7") sheets blue
  Fun Foam
- 4 rubber bands
- 2 large ornament hangers
- 2 small split-shot fishing
  weights
- Large plastic bucket for
  fish game
- Blue or green plastic
  wrap for water

1. Cover your work surface with waxed paper.

2. Spray-paint the dowels. (**Note:** Child will need help with this step.) Let the paint dry. Measure and mark each dowel at 9" intervals.

3. For each pole, to make the fishing line, glue 1 end of 1 ribbon length to 1 end of a dowel. Loop the ribbon and glue it at the marked points as shown at right. Let the glue dry.

4. For the handle, cover 1 side of 1 foam sheet with glue. Align 1 short edge of the foam with 1 end of the dowel as shown. Tightly roll the foam around the dowel. Wrap 2 rubber bands around the foam to hold it in place. Let the glue dry. Then remove the rubber bands.

5. To make the hook, tie 1 ornament hanger to the end of the ribbon tail. Attach a weight to the ribbon 3" from the hook. Repeat for the remaining pole.

6. Fill the bucket with the plastic wrap.

Go-Fish Rules

1. Arrange the fish on the wrap with their "mouths" facing upward.

2. Let the players take turns trying to hook a fish, using a pole.

3. The player who catches the most fish is the winner.

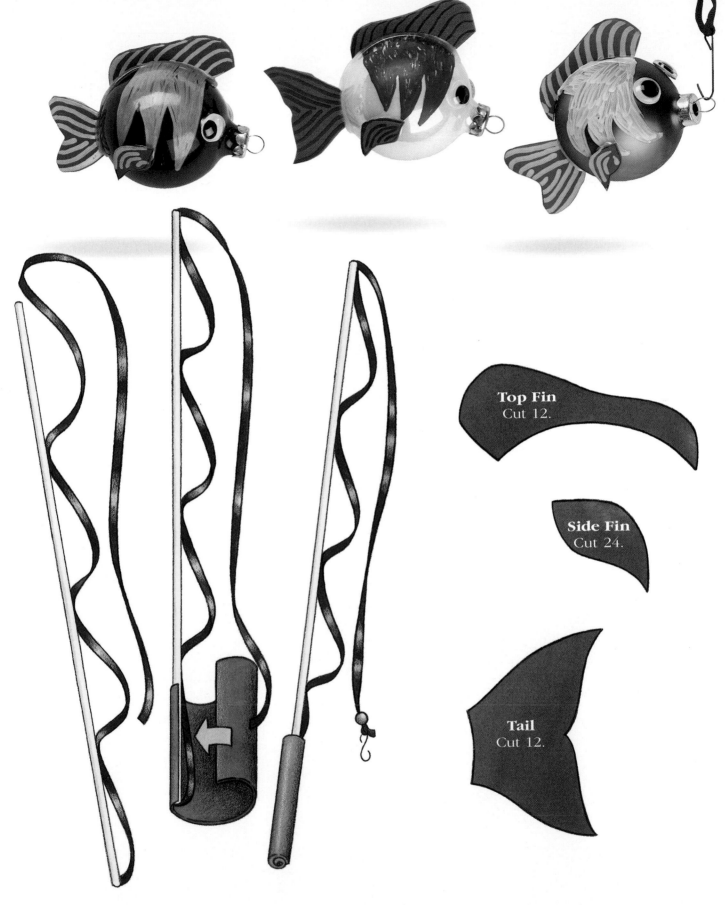

Top Fin
Cut 12.

Side Fin
Cut 24.

Tail
Cut 12.

North-Pole Finger Puppets

Help children create their own Christmas tale with these cheery mini puppets made from plush felt.

You will need (for each puppet):

- Patterns on page 53
- Tracing paper
- Pencil
- Scissors
- Ruler
- 2 (7-mm) wiggle eyes
- Thick craft glue

1. Trace the desired patterns. Cut them out. Transfer the patterns to the color of felt indicated. Cut out the puppet pieces.

2. **For Santa,** apply a thin line of glue along the sides and the top of 1 body piece. With the edges aligned, glue the 2 body pieces together, leaving the straight bottom edge open.

3. Glue Santa's beard/head onto the body, with the bottom of the beard 1¼" above the bottom edge of the body. Glue Santa's hat in place. Center and glue Santa's face just below the hat.

4. Glue the white pom-pom to the tip of the hat. Center and glue the black pom-poms on Santa's body. Glue the wiggle eyes on Santa's face, leaving ¼" between the eyes. Using the black marker, draw a smile just below the face. Let the glue dry before using the puppet.

5. **For Mrs. Santa,** refer to Step 2 to glue the body pieces together. Glue Mrs. Santa's hair/head on the body, with the bottom of the head 2" above the bottom edge of the body. Glue the face along the bottom of the head.

For Santa:
- 4" x 6" scrap red plush felt
- 3" x 3½" scrap white, 1½" x 3" scrap red, and 1½" x 2" scrap flesh-colored regular felt
- 1 (7-mm) white and 2 (5-mm) black pom-poms
- Fine-tip permanent black marker

For Mrs. Santa:
- 4" x 6" scrap red plush felt
- 2½" square white and 2" square flesh-colored regular felt
- 5 (5-mm) white pom-poms
- Fine-tip permanent black marker
- Pink cosmetic blush
- Cotton swab

51

For reindeer:
- 4" x 6" scrap tan plush felt
- 2½" x 3½" scrap tan regular felt
- 1 green pipe cleaner
- 1 (7-mm) red pom-pom

For snowman:
- 4" x 6" scrap white plush felt
- 1¾"-diameter circle white, 2" x 2½" scrap green, and 1½" square orange regular felt
- fine-tip permanent black marker
- 3 (5-mm) black pom-poms

6. Referring to the photograph, glue the wiggle eyes ⅜" from the top of the face, leaving ¼" between the eyes. Using the black marker, draw a smile on the face ¼" below the eyes. Glue the white pom-poms in a curve just below the face, spacing them evenly. Let the glue dry.

7. To make Mrs. Santa's cheeks, using the cotton swab, apply the blush to the face on each side of the mouth.

8. For the reindeer, cut the pipe cleaner in 2 (3") pieces. Fold each piece in half. Glue the bent pipe cleaners to the center top of 1 body piece, with the bent ends extending ½" beyond the edge of the felt as shown.

9. Referring to Step 2, glue the body pieces together, making sure that the pipe cleaners are sandwiched between the body pieces. Glue the head in place, with the bottom of the head 1¾" above the bottom edge of the body.

10. Glue the wiggle eyes ¾" above the bottom of the face, leaving ½" between the eyes. Glue the red pom-pom at the center bottom of the face. Let the glue dry before using the puppet.

11. For the snowman, refer to Step 2 to glue the body pieces together. Glue the 1¾"-diameter circle to the top of the body, with the bottom of the circle 2¼" above the bottom edge of the body.

12. Referring to the photograph, glue the hat on the top of the head, angling it slightly. Center and glue the wiggle eyes just below the hat, leaving ⅜" between the eyes. Glue the nose in place below the eyes, with the straight end centered between the eyes. Using the black marker, draw a smile on the head just below and to the right of the nose. Center and glue the black pom-poms in a row on the snowman body. Let the glue dry before using the puppet.

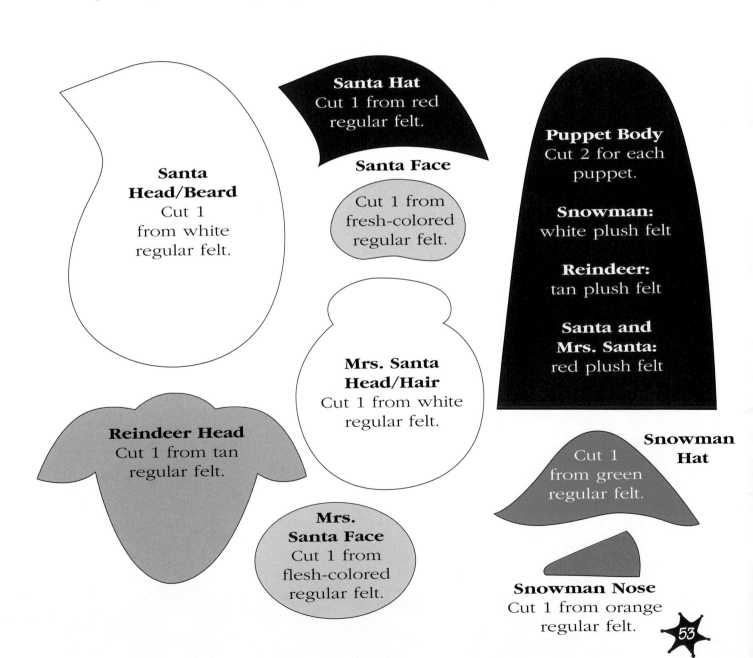

Santa Hat
Cut 1 from red
regular felt.

Santa Face
Cut 1 from
fresh-colored
regular felt.

Santa Head/Beard
Cut 1
from white
regular felt.

Puppet Body
Cut 2 for each
puppet.

Snowman:
white plush felt

Reindeer:
tan plush felt

Santa and Mrs. Santa:
red plush felt

Mrs. Santa Head/Hair
Cut 1 from white
regular felt.

Reindeer Head
Cut 1 from tan
regular felt.

Snowman Hat
Cut 1
from green
regular felt.

Mrs. Santa Face
Cut 1 from
flesh-colored
regular felt.

Snowman Nose
Cut 1 from orange
regular felt.

53

Party 'n' Things

Jumbo Candy Garland

Kids can drape their doorways with a gigantic candy garland. It's made with Styrofoam bowls and cellophane.

You will need:
- 20"-wide colored cellophane: 5 feet each blue, red, and green; 10 feet yellow
- 16 gold pipe cleaners
- 16 (12-ounce) Styrofoam bowls
- 32 twist ties
- 8" length rope

1. Cut the blue, red, and green cellophane into 4 (20" x 15") pieces each. Cut the yellow cellophane into 8 (20" x 15") pieces. Cut the pipe cleaners in half.

2. Stack 2 pieces of yellow cellophane on a flat surface. Place the base of 1 bowl in the center and wrap both pieces of cellophane over the bowl. Twist each end of the cellophane tightly and secure with a twist tie. Repeat with the rest of the yellow cellophane and 3 more bowls.

3. Use only 1 piece of cellophane to wrap each of the remaining bowls. Twist each end tightly and secure with a twist tie.

4. Lay the rope down on a flat surface. Beginning about 12" from 1 end of the rope, start attaching the "candy." Take 2 matching bowls and place the flat rim sides together, with the rope sandwiched in between them. To hold the bowls together and to attach them to the rope, wrap a pipe cleaner around the ends over the twist ties. Attach all the remaining bowls to the rope in the same manner.

You will need:

- Pattern on page 60
- Colored paper
- Scissors
- Colored markers
- Wiggle eyes (optional)
- Glue (optional)
- Circle stickers or clear tape

Party Invitation

If you're planning a Christmas party, Bert and Ernie have an invitation your child can use to spread the news.

1. Photocopy the pattern onto the colored paper.

2. Cut out the invitation.

3. Use the markers to fill in the party information and the address. Don't forget to color the designs.

4. Fold the invitation in half, with the star at the top as shown.

5. Fold the invitation again, bringing the address side forward. Unfold the invitation. Find the dot on the top of the letter R in the word "PARTY." From that point make a diagonal fold to the dot on the right of the star. Find the dot on the left of the star and make another diagonal fold. When you close the card, crease the fold in the star so that the point of the star folds down inside the card.

6. Color the eyes or glue wiggle eyes onto the star. If using glue, let dry.

7. Fold the invitation so that the address is on the outside. Fasten the invitation with a circle sticker or tape it closed to the right of the address.

59

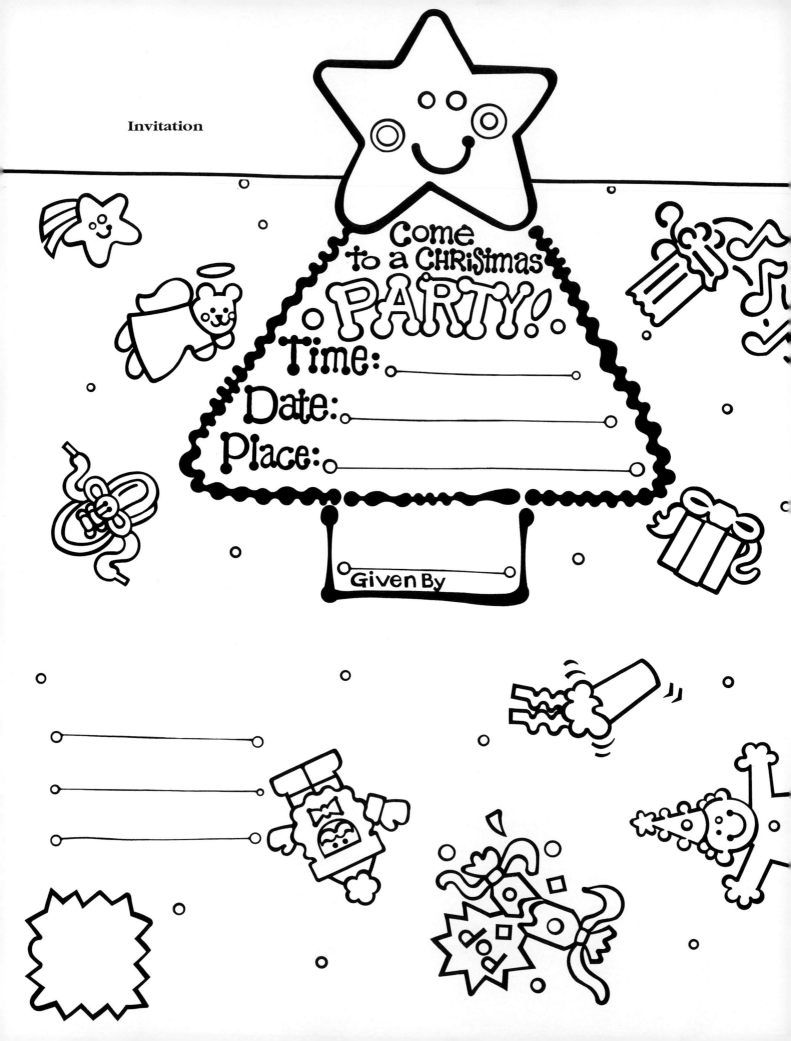

Invitation

Come to a CHRISTMAS PARTY!

Time:

Date:

Place:

Given By

Ho-Ho Hats

Fun to make and even more fun to wear, these pointy party hats make Elmo and party guests laugh and smile.

1. Glue pom-poms or hard candy all around the hat. Let the glue dry.

2. To top the hat, make a bow from the ribbon and glue it on or cut a star from the colored paper and glue it on. If using glue, let dry.

You will need (for each hat):
- Purchased party hat
- Assorted trims: colored pom-poms, hard candy, ribbon, colored paper
- Scissors
- Glue

Colorful Kazoos

Your child can play his or her favorite Christmas songs with this homemade musical instrument.

**You will need
(for each kazoo):**

- Glue
- 4½" x 6" piece corrugated paper
- 1 toilet-paper tube
- 1-pound coffee can
- Waxed paper
- Pencil
- Scissors
- Rubber band
- Curling ribbon

1. Glue the corrugated paper around the toilet-paper tube. Let the glue dry.

2. Stand the coffee can on the waxed paper and trace around it. Cut out the circle.

3. Place the wax paper circle over 1 end of the kazoo. Hold the paper in place with the rubber band.

4. To decorate, tie a piece of ribbon around the rubber band and curl the ends.

5. To play the kazoo, place the open end over your mouth and hum a tune.

Candy-Stick Christmas Vase

Cookie Monster knows that candy sticks are good for decorating. Kids can glue them around a coffee can for a striped vase.

1. Place the rubber bands around the coffee can, positioning 1 near the top and 1 near the bottom. Apply glue to 1 side of 1 candy stick. Slip the candy stick under the rubber bands, with the glue side toward the can. Continue in this manner until all the candy sticks have been used. Let the glue dry.

2. Remove the rubber bands. Tie the ribbon in a knot around the center of the candy-covered can. Fill the vase with water and flowers or a small potted Christmas tree.

You will need:
- 2 rubber bands
- 5"-diameter coffee can
- Thick craft glue
- Approximately 36 candy sticks
- 1 yard 1"-wide green polka-dot grosgrain ribbon
- Flowers or small Christmas tree

Holiday Tray

Once they tape the pattern to the bottom of a clear tray, kids can start painting. A see-through tray makes it easy for children to copy the candy canes.

You will need:

- Tracing paper
- Pencil
- Clear acrylic tray
- Masking tape
- Acrylic enamel paints: red, white, green
- Paintbrushes
- Clear acrylic spray sealer

1. Trace the pattern. Center the pattern facedown on the bottom of the tray. Tape it in place.

2. Turn the tray over. Beginning with the red stripes and letting the paint dry between colors, paint the candy canes red and white, as indicated on the pattern; paint the dots green. Remove the pattern.

3. Let dry overnight. Spray the back of the tray, using the acrylic sealer. (**Note:** Child will need help with this step.) Let the sealer dry.

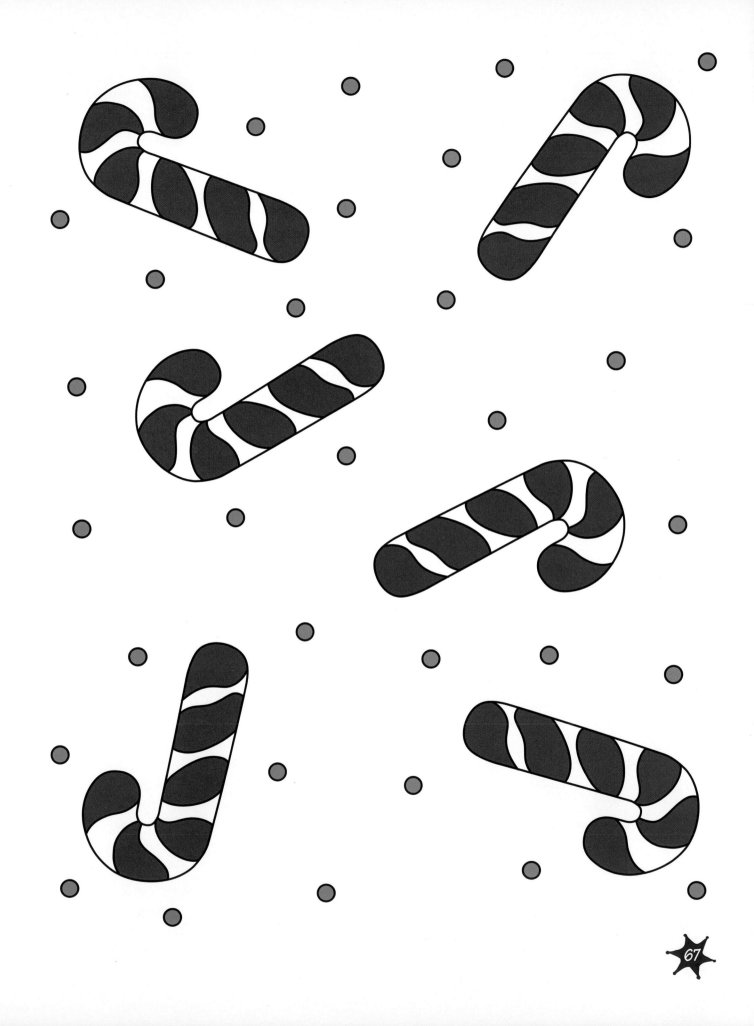

Treat Rolls

These colorful paper rolls hide a secret surprise inside.

You will need (for each roll):
- Scissors
- 1 toilet-paper tube
- Colored tissue paper
- Wrapping paper
- Ruler
- Pencil
- Glue stick
- Small toy, candy, and a greeting written on a strip of paper
- String

1. Cut the toilet-paper tube in half. Cut 2 (6" x 10") rectangles from tissue paper. Cut 1 (6½" x 9") rectangle from wrapping paper.

2. Put the 2 halves of the toilet-paper tube back together and treat them as 1 unit. Stack the 2 pieces of tissue paper. Center the tube unit along 1 long edge of the paper. Then roll the paper around the tube unit. The paper will extend beyond the ends of the tube. When you come to the edge of the paper, glue it in place, leaving the ends open. Let the glue dry.

3. Center the tissue paper-covered tube unit along 1 long edge of the wrapping paper. The ends of the tissue paper will extend beyond the wrapping paper. Roll the wrapping paper around the tissue-covered tube. Then glue the long edge in place, leaving the ends open. Let the glue dry.

4. Insert a small toy, some candy, and a greeting into the tube through 1 end.

5. Wrap the string 2 or 3 times around 1 end of the tube to cinch the paper. Pull the string as tight as you can without tearing the paper. Then remove the string and fringe the end of the paper with the scissors. Repeat for the remaining end.

6. To make your popper pop, hold 1 end in each hand and break the tube in half.

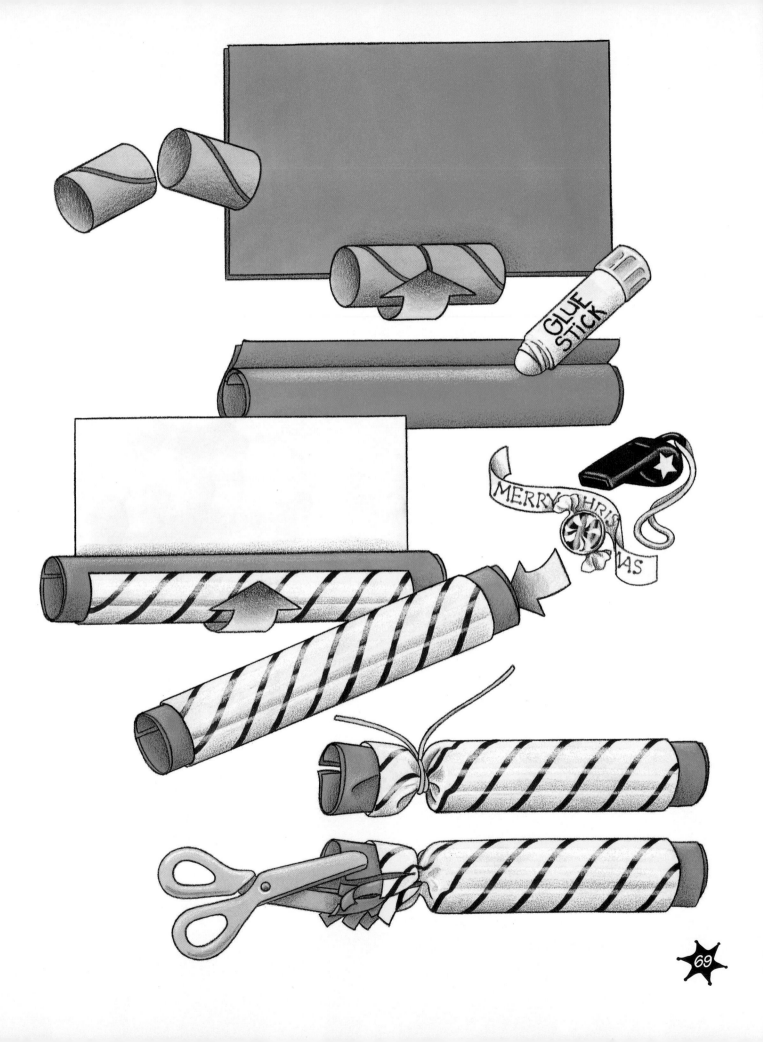

Presents to Make

Surprise Balls

It's a present. No, it's an ornament. Actually, it's both! Big Bird found these plastic ornaments at a crafts store—they come in all shapes and sizes. Kids like to fill them with colorful gifts.

**You will need
(for each ball):**

- Plastic ball ornament that opens
- Golf tees, embroidery floss, jacks and ball, or other small gifts
- Paper curling ribbon: red, green, gold

1. Decide who you want to give the ornament gift to and then choose a colorful gift. The balls shown here are filled with jacks for a young friend, embroidery floss for a stitcher, and tees for a golfer. There are lots of other possibilities, so use your imagination and have fun!

2. Cut a 12" piece each of red, green, and gold ribbon. Thread the ribbons through the opening at the top of the ornament and tie them in a knot. Carefully pull the edge of scissors across the ribbon to make it curl.

Dip-and-Drip Flowerpots

Kids can have fun with plain pots. Just dip the rims and then let the paint run!

1. Cover the work surface with the newspaper. Pour the paints into separate foil pans. The paint should be ¼" to ½" deep in each pan.

You will need:

- Newspaper
- Latex paints in desired colors
- Foil baking pans (1 for each color of paint)
- Assorted clay flowerpots

2. For the single-color pot,
turn the pot upside down and dip the rim into 1 color of paint. (The deeper you dip the pot, the wider the band of color will be.) Turn the pot right side up and let the paint run down the sides. (If the paint does not drip as much as you'd like, mix a little water into the paint and redip the pot.) Let the paint dry.

3. For the multicolored pot, complete Step 2. When the paint is dry, dip the pot into a different color of paint, making sure not to dip as much of the rim into the paint as the first time or the second layer of paint will cover the first layer. Turn the pot right side up and let the paint run down the sides. Let the paint dry. If desired, dip the pot into a third color, making sure not to dip as much of the rim as the second time. Let the paint dry.

4. For the marbleized-rim pot, swirl 1 color of paint into a pan of a different color of paint. Dip the rim of the pot into the pan so that it touches both colors of paint. Twist the pot to swirl the colors together on the rim. Turn the pot right side up and let the paint run down the sides. Let the paint dry.

You will need:

- Fabric paints: red, light blue, pink
- 3 paper plates
- 3 plaid dish towels
- Fine-point black fabric marker

Decorated Dish Towels

Bring on the dishes! With finger-painted towels like these, Elmo, Cookie Monster, and Oscar want to help with the cleanup after meals.

1. Pour each paint color onto a different paper plate.

2. Unfold the towels and lay them flat. Press your index finger into the paint. Then use your finger like a stamp and stamp 1 oval in each square across 1 end of the towel. (You may want to practice first on paper.) Stamp the same color shape across the other end of the towel. Wash your finger and dry it before changing colors. **For the ladybug,** use the red paint and make vertical ovals. **For the bird,** use blue paint and turn your finger sideways to make horizontal ovals. **For the pig,** use pink paint and make horizontal ovals. Let the paint dry.

3. **For the ladybug,** use the marker to add the markings on the back, the head, and the antennae. **For the bird,** add a beak, an eye, a wing, a tail, and legs. **For the pig,** draw ears, a tail, and legs and add details to the face.

4. To set the paint on the towels, follow the manufacturer's directions.

You will need
(for each balloon):

- Empty 16-ounce plastic shampoo bottle
- 1 heavy-duty (helium-quality latex) 11" balloon
- ½ to ¾ cup of flour
- Rag and dishcloth

Squish 'n' Wish

A child can give these to adults to reduce stress, and to friends to boost creative thinking—just squish them and make a wish.

Note: Children must be supervised at all times when working with balloons.

1. Thoroughly rinse the shampoo bottle with warm water until all soapsuds are gone. Cut off the bottom of the bottle. Dry the inside of the bottle thoroughly.

2. Roll down the neck of the balloon and stretch it over the bottle's neck. Make sure it fits tightly.

3. Scoop 2 tablespoons of flour into the bottle and shake the flour into the balloon. Continue adding a tablespoon of flour at a time until the balloon appears full. Gently press the balloon against the countertop to force any air out of the balloon. Add more flour. Continue pressing out air and filling the balloon with flour until it is the weight and has the feel you desire. (The more air inside, the more spongy the feel. Less air allows the balloon to be molded into shapes.)

4. When the balloon is filled, pinch it at the base of the neck and remove the bottle. Tie the neck into a knot. With a slightly damp rag, wipe off any excess flour around the outside of the bal-loon. Pat the balloon dry with the dishcloth.

Family Tree

Grover, Elmo, and Mr. Snuffleupagus learned about genealogy (that's the history of a family) by making a family tree. These make nice gifts for parents and grandparents, as well.

1. Trace and cut out the patterns.

2. Use the marker to trace the tree and apple patterns onto the sponge. Cut out the shapes.

You will need:

- Patterns on page 83
- Tracing paper
- Pencil
- Scissors
- Black fine-tip marker
- Kitchen sponge
- Paintbrush
- Tempera paint: brown, red
- 9" x 11" piece white construction paper
- Green stamp pad

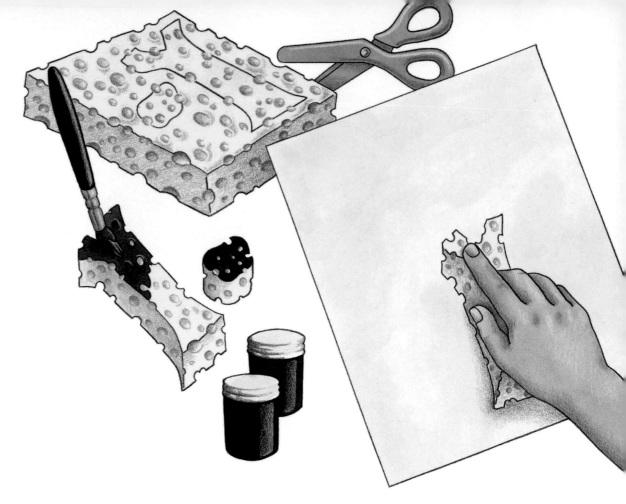

3. Use the paintbrush to paint 1 side of the tree-trunk sponge with brown. Press the painted side of the sponge onto the center of the white construction paper, with the bottom of the trunk about 1" from the bottom of the paper.

4. Paint 1 side of the apple sponge with red. Make a sponge-print apple for each member of the family, starting near the top of the tree with Mom and Dad (see the photograph and at right). You may need to repaint your apple sponge between making apples.

5. When the paint is dry, print a name beside each apple, using the marker. After labeling an apple for Mom and an apple for Dad, add the children's names according to age. Put the oldest child's name near the highest unmarked apple on the tree. Write the name of the youngest child near the apple closest to the ground.

6. To make the leaves, press your index finger onto the green stamp pad. Then use your inked finger to make fingerprint leaves. Make as many leaves as you want. Re-ink your fingertip if the leaves get too light. To make a darker leaf, ink your finger on the pad and make a second fingerprint leaf on top of one already on the tree.

7. When the ink is dry, use the marker to draw stems on the apples and to outline leaves that are near the stems (see the photograph and above). Print your family name neatly across the tree trunk near the base of the tree. Center and print "My Family Tree" below the tree.

Apple

Tree Trunk

Corrugated Frames

Just like Ernie, your child will love seeing his or her picture or a friend's inside one of these colorful corrugated picture frames.

You will need:

- Posterboard in assorted colors
- Yardstick
- Ruler
- Pencil
- Scissors
- Glue
- Paper clips
- Photographs
- Corrugated scalloped border
- Corrugated paper in assorted colors
- Scraps of corrugated fence border

Scalloped Frame

1. For a 5" x 7" photograph, measure and mark a 7" x 28" rectangle on the back of the desired posterboard. Cut out.

2. On the back of the rectangle, measure and mark 4" from 1 short end. Draw a line across the posterboard at this mark. Measure 10" from this line and draw another line. Then draw another line 10" from the second line.

3. Fold and crease the posterboard along each line.

4. Unfold the rectangle. Find the center of one of the 7" x 10" areas. Center the photograph on the right side of this area and glue it in place. Let the glue dry. With your ruler and pencil, measure and draw a line ½" from the right side and ½" from the left side of the photograph.

5. Fold and crease the rectangle along the creased lines again. Glue the posterboard ends together where they overlap. Hold them in place with paper clips until the glue dries.

6. Cut 2 (11") matching strips from the scalloped border. Glue 1 strip down each side of the frame on the lines (ends will extend ½" beyond the the top and the bottom of the frame).

7. Cut 2 (9½") strips from the scalloped border. Place 1 strip across the top of the frame, lining it up the scallops at the corners. Trim the corners of the side strips so that the scallop design continues around the corner of the frame. Repeat for the bottom strip. Glue the strips in place. Let the glue dry.

Two-Color Frame

1. For a 3½" x 5" or 4" x 6" photograph, measure and mark an 8" x 21½" rectangle on the back of the desired posterboard. Cut out.

2. Measure and mark 4½" from 1 short end of the rectangle. Draw a line across the posterboard at this mark. Measure 6¼" from this line and draw another line. Then draw another line 6¼" from the second line.

3. Fold and crease the posterboard along each line. Glue the ends of the posterboard together where they overlap. Hold them in place with paper clips until the glue dries.

4. Cut an 8" x 6½" rectangle from the desired corrugated paper.

5. On the back of the corrugated paper, place the photograph in the center and trace it. Inside this outline, draw another line, following the next row of dots on the paper. Cut along this inside line to make a window for the photograph.

6. Glue the corrugated paper frame to the front of the posterboard along 3 sides. Leave 1 side open so that the photograph can be slipped in and out.

7. To decorate the frame, use scraps of the corrugated fence-border strips. Glue the border strips to the front of the corrugated frame.

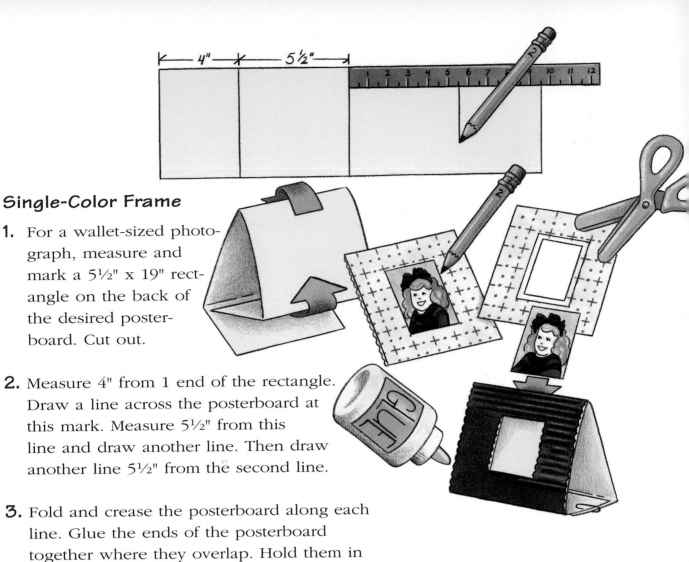

Single-Color Frame

1. For a wallet-sized photo-graph, measure and mark a 5½" x 19" rect-angle on the back of the desired poster-board. Cut out.

2. Measure 4" from 1 end of the rectangle. Draw a line across the posterboard at this mark. Measure 5½" from this line and draw another line. Then draw another line 5½" from the second line.

3. Fold and crease the posterboard along each line. Glue the ends of the posterboard together where they overlap. Hold them in place with paper clips until the glue dries.

4. Cut a 5½" x 5¾" piece from the desired cor-rugated paper.

5. On the back of the corrugated paper, place the photograph in the center and trace it. Inside this outline, draw another line, fol-lowing the next row of dots on the paper. Cut along this inside line to make a window for the photograph.

6. Glue the corrugated paper frame to the front of the posterboard along 3 sides. Leave 1 side open so that the photograph can be slipped in and out.

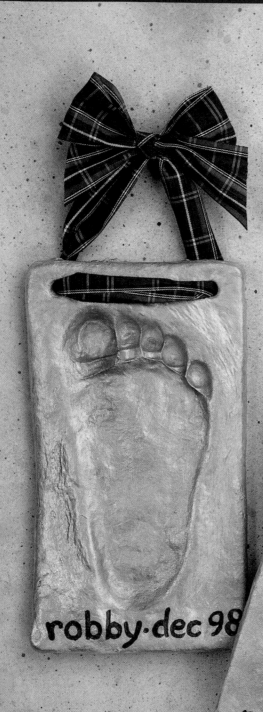

Permanent Prints

Children can craft keepsakes with these decorative molds. Elmo thinks they are a hands-down favorite.

1. Preheat the oven to 250°. (**Note:** Child will need help with this step.)

2. Mix the flour and the salt in a bowl. Slowly add a little water. Using your hands, shape the mixture into a soft dough ball, adding more water as necessary. Divide the ball in half and roll out each half onto a floured piece of foil. Flour the top of each dough piece. Press a hand into 1 piece and a foot into the other.

3. With the toothpick, cut around the prints, leaving a border around the edges (see the photograph). Make a hole in each top corner, ½" from each side edge.

4. Bake each print for 2 hours. Then turn them over and bake 1 hour longer. Let them cool thoroughly.

5. Dust off the excess flour on both sides of each print. Mix 1 part gold paint and 2 parts varnish. With the paintbrush, paint both sides of each print, letting 1 side dry before painting the other. Let the paint dry.

6. Using the red paint pen, write your name and the date across the bottom of each print. Let the paint dry.

7. Referring to the photograph, thread 1 ribbon length through each pair of holes. Tie the ends of each length in a bow.

You will need:
- 2 cups all-purpose flour
- ½ cup salt
- Medium-sized bowl
- Water
- Foil
- Toothpick
- Gold liquid acrylic paint
- Clear acrylic varnish
- Medium paintbrush
- Red paint pen
- 2 (22") lengths 1½"-wide ribbon

Wrap It Up

Holly-Jolly Gift Wrap

The Honker loves it when his friends make crinkled wrapping paper from purchased paper twists. Add a few big jingle bells to complete a berry-best package.

**You will need
(for both styles):**

- Pattern at right
- Pencil
- Tracing paper
- Scissors
- Twisted paper rolls: red, green
- Transparent tape
- Thick craft glue
- 12 (¾"-diameter) red jingle bells

1. Using the pencil, transfer the holly-leaf pattern onto the tracing paper. Cut out the pattern.

2. Cut a length of red twisted paper several inches longer than the package you are wrapping. Untwist the paper and smooth it so that it is almost flat. (If the paper is not wide enough to cover your package, cut another length equal to the first length. Smooth this length until it is almost flat and

then piece the 2 sheets of paper by overlapping 1 long edge of each sheet slightly and taping them together.) Wrap your package. Set the wrapped package aside.

3. Cut a 6" length of green twisted paper. Untwist the paper and smooth it as before. Using the pencil, transfer the holly-leaf pattern to 1 (6") edge of the paper. To cut several leaves at once, with the traced pattern on top, accordion-fold the paper several times. Cut out the pattern through all the layers of the green twisted paper. You will need 5 holly leaves for each package shown in the photograph.

4. **For the large package,** referring to the photograph, glue 2 pairs of leaves and 1 single leaf to the top of the package. Glue 3 jingle bells to 1 tip of the single holly leaf. Glue 3 jingle bells to each pair where the points meet.

5. **For the small package,** cut a length of green twisted paper long enough to wrap around the length of the package. Untwist the paper and cut it in half lengthwise to make 2 long strips. Retwist each strip. Referring to the photograph, wrap 1 strip lengthwise around the package, taping the cut ends to the center top of the package. Wrap the remaining strip widthwise around the package, taping as before. Referring to the photograph, glue 3 holly leaves on 1 side of the package top. Glue 2 holly leaves on the opposite side. Glue 3 jingle bells to the center of the package where the points of the leaves meet.

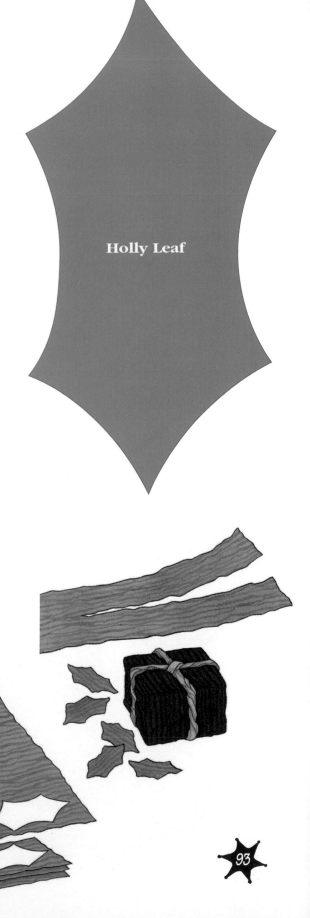

Holly Leaf

You will need (for each box):

- Scissors
- Liquid ravel preventer
- Glue

For the automobile box:

- Red rectangular box
- 1"-wide black-and-white striped grosgrain ribbon
- Assorted automobile and party-hat stickers

It's a Stick Up!

These packages bring smiles even before the gifts inside are revealed! Kids can add personality plus to ordinary boxes with colorful stickers, rickrack, and ribbon.

Automobile Box

1. Before you begin, measure across the top and the bottom of the box to determine how much ribbon you will need. Cut 2 strips of ribbon to fit. Apply liquid ravel preventer to the cut ends of the ribbon and let dry. Glue the corresponding lengths along the top and bottom edges of the box top as shown.

2. Place the automobile stickers between the ribbon strips. Add the hat stickers as desired.

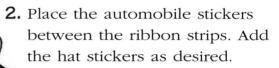

Tree Box

1. Center and apply the tree sticker diagonally on the box top.

2. Cut the rickrack into 2 strips, each slightly longer than the width of the tree. Glue them across the tree (see the photograph).

3. Decorate the tree with the star and ornament stickers as desired. Arrange the remaining stars around the tree as desired.

4. Tie the ribbon in a bow and glue it to the top of the tree. Let the glue dry.

For the tree box:
- White square box
- Large tree sticker
- 1/4"-wide yellow rick-rack scraps
- Assorted star and ornament stickers
- 1/2 yard 3/8"-wide red-and-white polka-dot grosgrain ribbon

Perky Reindeer Wrap

Elmo imitates the face of a reindeer with dried beans, a red candy heart, and kraft paper. Small twigs look like antlers.

You will need:
- Patterns at right
- Pencil
- Tracing paper
- Scissors
- Brown kraft paper
- Black construction paper
- Wrapped gift
- Craft glue
- Twigs
- Dried beans
- Red candy hearts

For the gift card:
- Wrapping paper to match the present

1. Trace the patterns and transfer them to the kraft paper. Cut out. Cut 4 strips from the construction paper for legs.

2. Glue the leg strips to the present. Glue the body over the top of the leg strips. Place the point of the head over the point of the body as shown. Before the glue dries, slide the twigs under the head along the top edge.

3. To make the face, glue on the dried beans for the eyes and a candy heart for the nose. Let the glue dry.

4. **For the gift card,** cut a square or rectangle from the wrapping paper and fold it in half. Repeat steps 1 and 3 to make the reindeer face only.

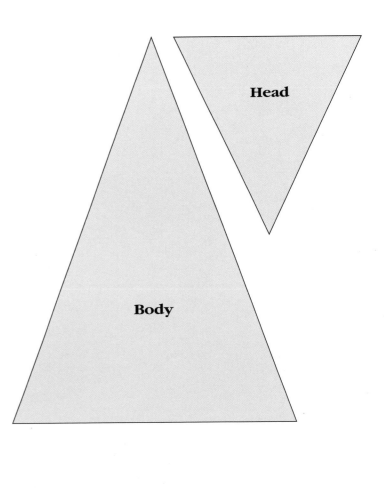

Head

Body

Shiny Shapes

These bags may look like decorations, but a present hides inside each vinyl package. Kids can draw simple holiday shapes—like Big Bird is doing—or dream up their own.

1. Choose a small gift to wrap.

2. Stack the vinyl rectangles together. On the top one, use the marker to draw one of the simple shapes shown here, such as a tree, a stocking, or a star, or draw your own shape. Just make sure the shape is large enough to hold the gift.

3. Cut out the 2 shapes at the same time along the drawn lines. Hold the 2 layers of vinyl together and punch holes about 1" apart all around the edges of the shape.

**You will need
(for each wrap):**
- 2 (11"x 17") pieces clear lightweight vinyl
- Permanent marker
- Scissors
- Hole punch
- Glue

For the tree:
- 14 buttons in various shapes and colors
- 2 yards red curling ribbon
- Green tissue paper

99

For the star:

- Gold glitter paint stick
- Yellow star stickers
- 3 yards yellow curling ribbon
- Dark blue tissue paper

For the stocking:

- 20" length green jumbo rickrack
- 2 yards green curling ribbon
- Red tissue paper

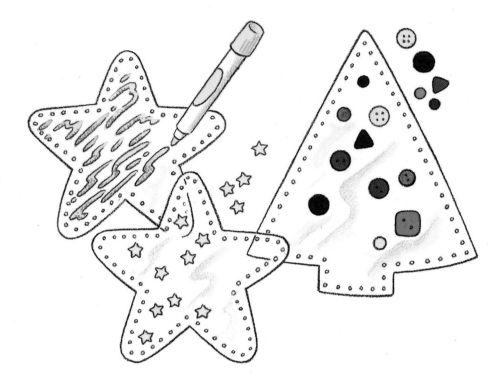

4. **For the tree,** glue on buttons to the front of the shape. Let the glue dry. **For the star,** decorate 1 side with glitter paint. Let the glue dry. Place star stickers on the other side of the star. **For the stocking,** glue pieces of rickrack on the toe, the heel, and the cuff on the front of the shape. Let the glue dry.

5. Slip the ribbon through the center bottom hole in the vinyl shape. Match the cut ends of the ribbon. Thread 1 end of the ribbon in the adjacent hole and then loop it around the edge of the shape. Keep threading and looping in this manner until you are halfway up the side. Then take the other end of the ribbon and loop it halfway up the other side of the shape.

6. To fill the shape with color, fold the tissue paper in half and stuff it inside the vinyl shape. Hide the small gift inside the tissue paper.

7. Continue looping the ribbon ends through the holes until you reach the top of the shape. Then tie the ribbon ends in a bow.

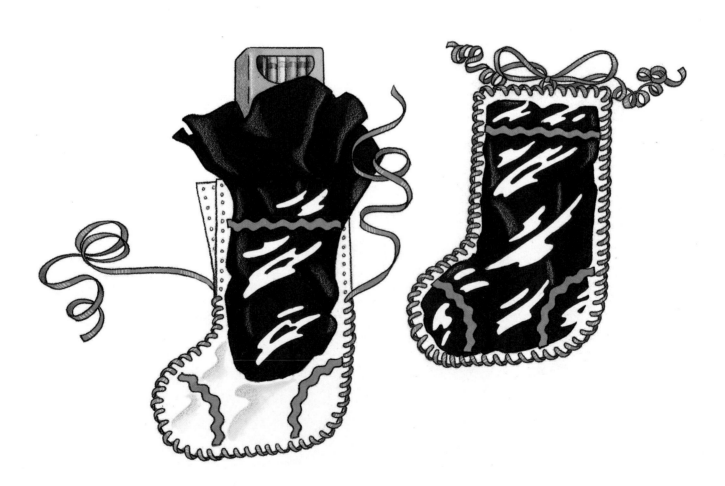

Awesome Ornaments

Color Melts

These ornaments resemble stained glass, but they're actually made from crayon shavings melted between waxed paper. Kids can hold the shapes up to a sunny window and watch the light filter through the colors.

**You will need
(for each ornament):**

- Tracing paper
- Pencil
- Scissors
- Heavyweight colored paper
- Masking tape
- Waxed paper
- Ironing board
- 2 cloth towels
- Crayons in desired colors
- Vegetable peeler
- Iron
- Glue
- Hole punch
- Scrap of satin ribbon

1. Trace and cut out the desired pattern (see pages 106–107). Fold the heavyweight paper in half. Transfer the pattern to the doubled paper.

2. Tape the 2 layers of the paper together to hold them in place. Cut along the inner and the outer edges of the design. Set the 2 shapes aside.

3. Repeat steps 1 and 2 with the waxed paper, cutting along the outer edge only. Do not tape the layers together.

4. Cover the ironing board with 1 towel. Place 1 waxed-paper cutout on the towel. Remove the paper from the crayons. Using the peeler, shave different colored crayons onto the waxed paper, lightly covering the surface. (Be careful not to make a pile of shavings or your ornament will appear dark.) Aligning the edges, place the remaining waxed-paper cutout on top of the first, sandwiching the shavings in between.

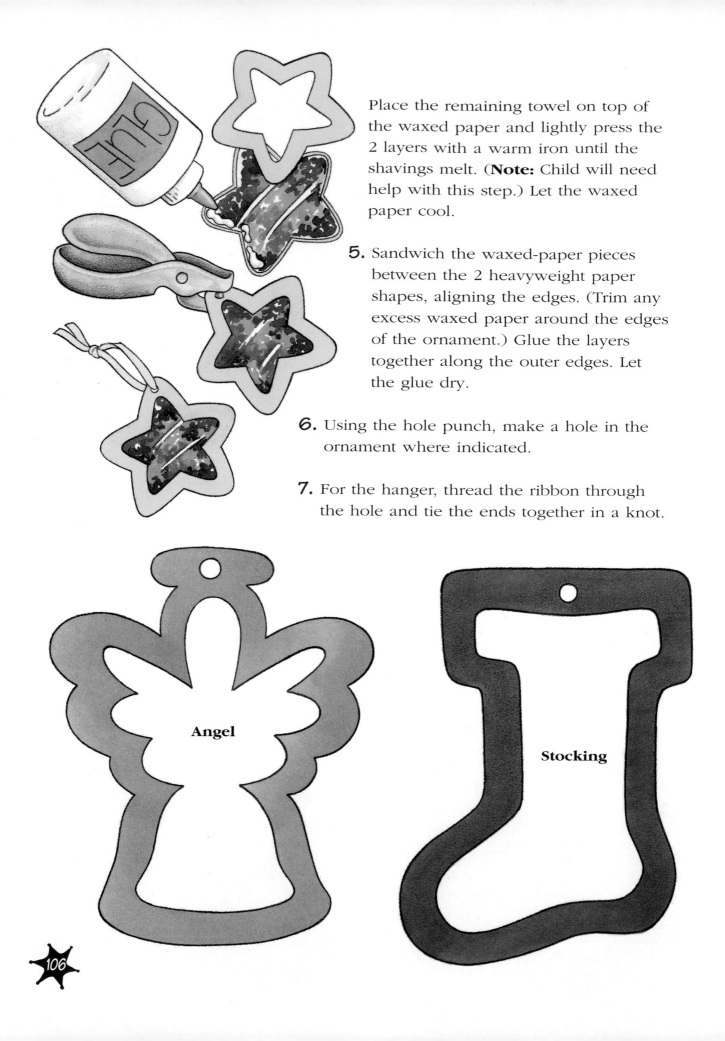

Place the remaining towel on top of the waxed paper and lightly press the 2 layers with a warm iron until the shavings melt. (**Note:** Child will need help with this step.) Let the waxed paper cool.

5. Sandwich the waxed-paper pieces between the 2 heavyweight paper shapes, aligning the edges. (Trim any excess waxed paper around the edges of the ornament.) Glue the layers together along the outer edges. Let the glue dry.

6. Using the hole punch, make a hole in the ornament where indicated.

7. For the hanger, thread the ribbon through the hole and tie the ends together in a knot.

Angel

Stocking

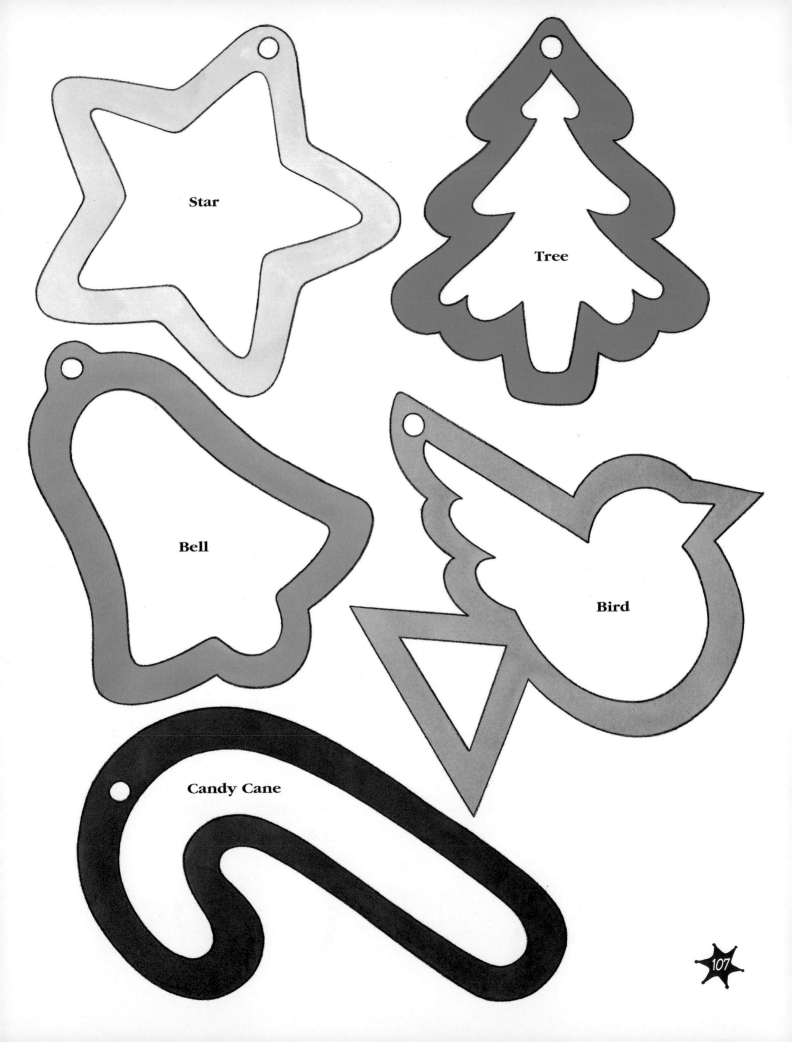

Star

Tree

Bell

Bird

Candy Cane

You will need (for 1 cone):

- Newspaper
- Paper cup
- Scissors
- Sugar cone
- Tissue paper in desired color
- Disposable pie pan
- Measuring spoons
- Craft glue
- Water
- 1 (2¼"-diameter) Styrofoam ball
- Glitter
- Scraps of ¼"-wide ribbon in color to match tissue paper

Dream Cones

Help kids turn real ice-cream sugar cones into ornaments for the tree.

1. Cover your work surface with newspaper. To make a working stand for the cone, turn the paper cup upside down on a flat surface. Cut a small hole in the bottom of the cup and then press the tip of the cone into the hole.

2. Tear the tissue paper into small pieces. In the pan, mix 3 tablespoons of glue with 3 tablespoons of water.

3. Dip a piece of tissue paper into the glue mixture and smooth it onto the ball. Continue adding tissue, overlap pieces as you work, until the ball is completely covered. While the tissue is still wet with glue, sprinkle glitter over the ball. Shake off excess glitter over newspaper. Let the ball dry.

4. Spread glue around the inside and top edges of the sugar cone. Gently press the ball into the cone. Let the glue dry.

5. Tie a small bow and glue it to the front of the cone. To make a hanger, fold a short length of ribbon in half and glue the ends to the top of the ball. Let the glue dry.

Shining Star Ornament

Twiddlebugs teach basic weaving with metallic floss and craft sticks. Then they glue on a sparkling gemstone for a jewel of a Christmas ornament.

**You will need
(for 1 ornament):**
- 2 wooden craft sticks
- Tacky glue
- DMC embroidery floss: purple #333, green #700
- Kreinik metallic floss: purple #012HL, green #008
- Scissors
- ¾" square acrylic jewel in desired color

1. Place 1 craft stick on top of the other and form a cross. Glue the sticks together. Let the glue dry.

2. Handle 6 strands of 1 color of embroidery floss and 1 strand of the same color of metallic floss as 1 unit. Wrap the floss over and around each stick as shown, working clockwise. Continue in this manner until the desired width of that color is achieved. Cut the floss and glue the ends to the back to secure. Let the glue dry. Repeat with the remaining color of floss, wrapping until the floss is ½" from the ends of each stick. Glue a jewel in the center of the floss. Let the glue dry.

3. For the hanger, cut a 6" length of floss in the desired color. Fold the length in half and glue the cut ends to the back of 1 stick.

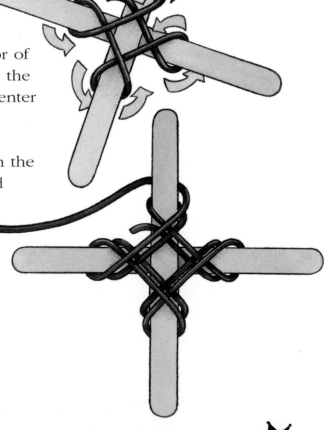

Oodles of Noodles

Macaroni comes in lots of shapes and sizes. When it's glued together and painted, it's fun for friends to guess what these ornaments are made of.

Wagon-Wheel Tree

**You will need
(for the tree):**

- Waxed paper
- Founder's Adhesive glue
- 11 wagon-wheel macaronis
- Green spray paint
- 10 small red decorative balls
- 6" length gold thread

1. Cover your work surface with waxed paper. To form the tree, refer to the photograph and glue the wagon wheels together in rows as follows: Start with Row 1, which has only 1 wheel. Glue 2 wheels together for Row 2. Glue 3 wheels together for Row 3. Glue 4 wheels together for Row 4. Then glue the 4 rows together as shown. For the tree trunk, glue 1 wheel at the center of the bottom row. Let the glue dry.

2. Spray-paint both sides of the tree, letting 1 side dry before painting the other. (**Note:** Child will need help with this step.) Be sure to do this outside or in a well-ventilated room. Let the paint dry.

3. Glue 1 red ball in the center of each wheel in rows 1–4.

4. To make a hanger, slip the gold thread through the top opening in the top wheel and knot the ends of the thread.

**You will need
(for the wreath):**
- Waxed paper
- Founder's Adhesive glue
- 7 bow-tie macaroni
- 4 small egg bow macaroni
- Spray paints: green, red
- Gold glitter paint
- 6" thread gold thread

Bow-Tie Wreaths

1. Cover your work surface with waxed paper. Glue 6 bow-tie macaronis together in a circle, slightly overlapping their edges. Let the glue dry.

2. Spray-paint the wreath green. (**Note:** Child will need help with this step.) Let the paint dry. For the bows, spray-paint the remaining bow tie and the small egg bow macaronis red. Let the paint dry.

3. Glue the large red bow to the top of the wreath, overlapping 2 green macaronis as shown.

4. Glue 1 small red bow to the center of each remaining green bow.

5. Dot the center of the red bows with glitter paint.

6. For a hanger, fold the gold thread in half and glue the ends to the top back of the wreath. Let the glue dry.

Glitter Balls

These shiny balls sparkle on the Christmas tree. And best of all, they won't break in small hands like glass balls can!

1. Cover the work surface with waxed paper.

2. For the hanger loop, push the paper clip into the top of the Styrofoam ball until just ¼" of the paper clip remains outside the ball.

3. Squirt a blob of glitter paint onto the paper plate. Use the paintbrush to apply the glitter paint to the ball. Let the paint dry. Apply a second coat of glitter paint if desired. Let the paint dry.

4. Tie the ribbon in a bow. Glue the bow to the top of the ornament in front of the hanger loop. Trim the ribbon ends. Let the glue dry.

You will need (for 1 ornament):
- Waxed paper
- Paper clip
- Styrofoam ball of desired size
- Glitter paint
- Paper plate
- Paintbrush
- ½ yard wire-edged ribbon
- Scissors
- Thick craft glue

Christmas Greetings

Greetings from Santa

This Santa flips his paper beard to reveal a Christmas message. Kids can make these to mail or to use as invitations or gift tags.

You will need:
- Tracing paper
- Pencil
- Scissors
- Construction paper: red, white, black, pink
- Fine-point black marker
- Glue stick
- White pom-pom

1. Trace and cut out the patterns.

2. From the red paper, cut out 1 triangle and 2 cheeks.

3. Fold the white paper in half. Place the beard pattern on the fold and cut 1. Also cut the hatband from a single layer of the white paper.

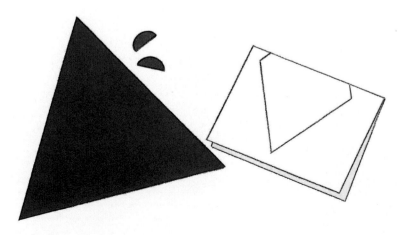

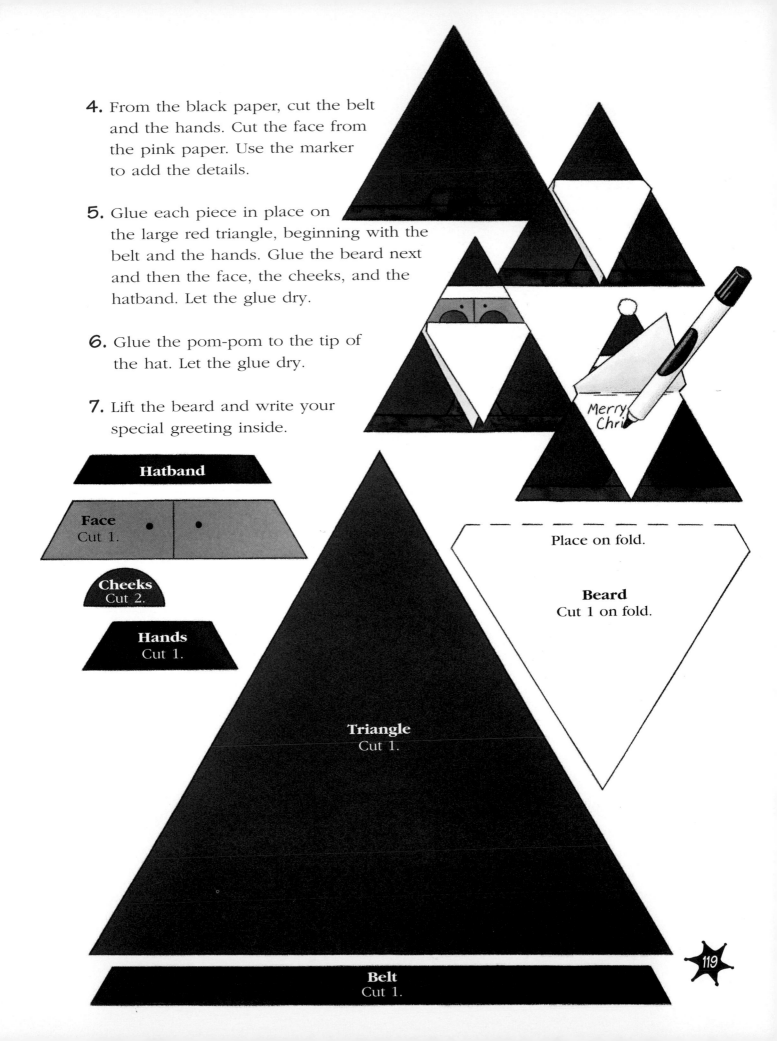

4. From the black paper, cut the belt and the hands. Cut the face from the pink paper. Use the marker to add the details.

5. Glue each piece in place on the large red triangle, beginning with the belt and the hands. Glue the beard next and then the face, the cheeks, and the hatband. Let the glue dry.

6. Glue the pom-pom to the tip of the hat. Let the glue dry.

7. Lift the beard and write your special greeting inside.

Hatband

Face
Cut 1.

Cheeks
Cut 2.

Hands
Cut 1.

Triangle
Cut 1.

Place on fold.

Beard
Cut 1 on fold.

Merry Chri

119

Belt
Cut 1.

Impression Cards

The shiny surface of these postcards looks like silver, but Zoe knows that it's really aluminum foil. Children can draw a winter scene to make their own Christmas postcards.

**You will need
(for each card):**

- Newspaper
- 4" x 6" piece heavy-duty aluminum foil
- Dull pencil
- Black ink
- Paintbrush
- Paper towel
- Glue
- 4½" x 6½" piece mat board in desired color
- Permanent marker

1. Fold several sheets of newspaper to make a padded work surface.

2. Place the foil on the newspaper. Using the dull pencil, draw a design.

3. Paint 1 coat of black ink over the drawing. Using the paper towel, gently wipe off the excess ink. Let the ink dry.

4. Glue the foil in the center of the mat board. Write your greeting on the back of the postcard, using the marker.

Star Card

Christmas Lights Card

Merry Christmas in Stitches

Children ages five and up can hand-sew these cards with bright yarns and a plastic darning needle.

You will need
(for each card):

- Patterns on page 125
- 3 sheets typing paper
- Scissors
- Craft glue
- Pencil
- ¼"-diameter hole punch
- Plastic yarn darning needle
- Transparent tape

Star Card

1. From the typing paper, cut 1 (4¼" x 5¾") piece for the inside sheet and 1 (4½" x 6") piece for the pattern tracing sheet.

2. Center the inside sheet on 1 (4½" x 6") piece of blue posterboard. With the edges aligned, glue 1 short edge of the inside sheet to the posterboard. This is the card back.

3. Using the hole punch, punch holes in the remaining blue posterboard piece where indicated on the pattern. Fold the same piece along the fold line indicated on the pattern. This is the card front.

4. Trace the star pattern onto the tracing sheet. Cut out the pattern. Transfer the pattern to the 2" x 3" yellow posterboard piece. Cut out the shape.

5. Thread the needle with the yellow yarn. Tape the bottom end of the yarn to the back of the card front at Hole 1. Referring to the pattern, stitch in the following order, keeping the yarn taut as you sew: up in Hole 1, down in Hole 2; up in Hole 1, down in Hole 3; up in Hole 1, down in Hole 4; continue in this manner to stitch in holes 5 to 9. Trim the yarn end and tape the end to the back of the card front at Hole 9.

6. Glue the top point of the star on top of Hole 1. Place the card front faceup on the card back, with the inside sheet between the 2 card pieces. Staple the cards together along the top edge. Cut a 9½" length of blue plaid ribbon. Wrap the ribbon length around the top of the card, covering the staples, and overlap the ends in back. Glue the ribbon in place. Tie the remaining ribbon in a bow. Glue the bow to the center front of the card, above the top point of the star.

For the star card:
- Posterboard: 2 (4½" x 6") pieces blue and 1 (2" x 3") piece yellow
- 64" length yellow yarn
- Stapler
- 19½" length ⅜"-wide blue plaid ribbon

For the Christmas-lights card:

- Posterboard: 2 (4½" x 6") pieces white; 3" square black; 1 (2") square each red, yellow, green, and blue
- 30" length green yarn

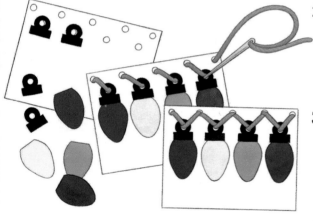

Christmas-Lights Card

1. Complete steps 1 and 2 for the star card, using 1 (4½" x 6") white posterboard piece. Trace the light bulb and top piece patterns onto the tracing sheet. Using the hole punch, punch a hole in the top piece pattern where indicated. Cut out the patterns. Transfer the top piece pattern 4 times to the 3" square black posterboard, marking the hole placement on each. Punch holes in the top pieces at the marks. Transfer the light-bulb pattern once each to the red, yellow, green, and blue posterboard squares. Cut out the shapes.

2. Punch holes in 1 long edge of both white posterboard pieces where indicated on the pattern. Fold 1 white piece along the fold line indicated on the pattern. This is the card front.

3. Glue the top pieces to the card front so that the top piece holes align with holes 2, 4, 6, and 8 on the card front. Glue 1 light bulb beneath each top piece.

4. Place the card front faceup on the card back, with the top holes aligned and the inside sheet between the 2 card pieces. Thread the needle with the green yarn. Stitch in the following order, keeping the yarn taut as you sew: up in Hole 1, leaving a 4" tail, and down in Hole 2; up in Hole 3, down in Hole 4; up in Hole 5, down in Hole 6; up in Hole 7, down in Hole 8; up in Hole 9, down in Hole 8; up in Hole 7, Hole 6; up in Hole 5, down in Hole 4; up in Hole 3, down in Hole 2. After the final stitch through Hole 2, tie the yarn ends together in a knot. Tape the knot to the back of the card back. Trim the excess.

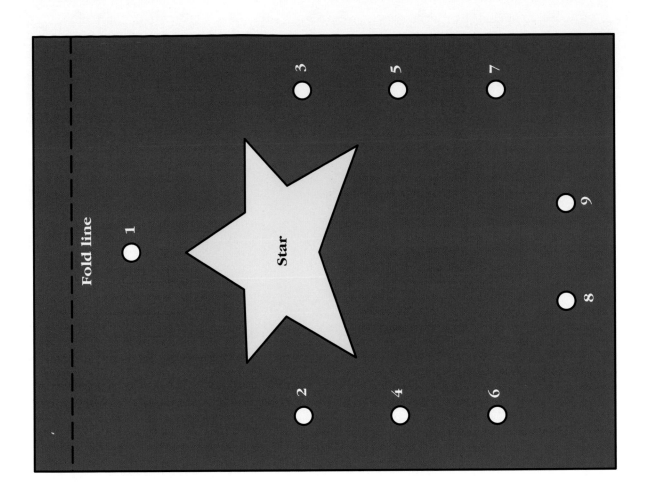

Fold line

1

3

5

7

Star

9

8

2

4

6

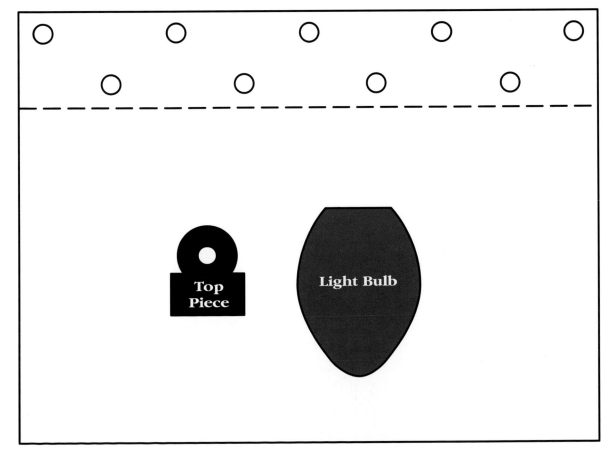

Top
Piece

Light Bulb

You will need (for each tag):

- Pencil
- 1 sheet Fun Foam in desired color
- Craft glue
- ½"-diameter pom-poms in desired colors
- Scissors
- Hole punch
- 24" length jumbo rickrack or ½"-wide grosgrain ribbon in desired color

Pom-pom Gift Tags

With these gift tags, a child can add a name to any package—even Big Bird's.

1. Using the pencil, print the desired name on the Fun Foam, making sure to leave a little space between each letter.

2. Trace the first letter with glue. Position pom-poms in the glue to form the shape of the letter. Continue in this manner with the remaining letters. Let the glue dry.

3. Very lightly draw a rectangle on the Fun Foam around the pom-pom name, making sure that each edge of the rectangle is at least 1" from the pom-pom name. Referring to the photograph, make 1 short end of the rectangle come to a point. Cut out the gift tag.

4. Punch a hole in 1 short end of the gift tag. Thread the rickrack or the ribbon through the hole. Tie the gift tag to the package.

Grin and Wear It

Merry Mittens

Here comes Santa Claus! And wherever the lucky wearer goes, he'll go, too!

1. Trace the patterns onto the tracing paper. Cut out.

2. Transfer 2 beards to the white plush felt and 2 faces to the pink felt. Cut out. Cut out 2 (3/8"-diameter) circles from the red felt for the noses.

3. Referring to the photograph, glue 1 face piece to the center back of each mitten. Glue 1 beard around each face piece. Glue 1 nose and 2 eyes to each face piece.

4. Glue 1 pom-pom to the center top of each mitten. Let the glue dry.

You will need:
- Tracing paper
- Pencil
- Scissors
- 4" x 6½" piece white plush felt
- Felt scraps: pink, red
- Flexible fabric glue
- 1 pair red mittens
- 4 (10-mm) wiggle eyes
- 2 (1") white pom-poms

Note: It may be necessary to adjust the pattern to fit the size of your mittens.

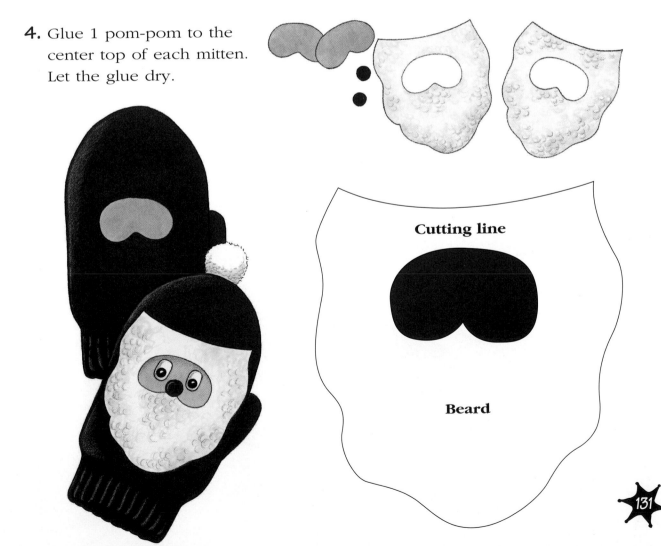

Cutting line

Beard

131

Party Shoes

Children can have a hand in decorating a pair of plain tennis shoes for the holidays. Zoe is getting ready to put on her dancing shoes.

1. Glue the plastic shapes onto the shoes. Let the glue dry.

2. Using fabric paint, make a simple design, such as a star, a heart, or a tree, on the shoe. Let the paint dry.

3. Remove the shoelaces. Cut the ribbon in half. Lace 1 length of ribbon in each shoe. String 1 bell onto each ribbon end. Then knot the ends.

You will need:

- 1 pair purchased canvas shoes
- Founder's Adhesive glue
- Craft stick
- Plastic holiday buttons and trims: stars, candy canes
- Fabric paint
- 1¾ yards ⅜-wide striped grosgrain ribbon
- 4 (½") jingle bells

You will need
(for each apron):
- Pattern at right
- Tracing paper
- Pencil
- Craft knife
- 1 sheet stencil plastic
- 1 purchased red canvas apron
- Masking tape
- Newspaper
- Green fabric paint
- Paper plate
- 1" foam paintbrush
- Assortment of buttons and pom-poms
- Tacky glue

Workshop Aprons

Before Santa's helpers scoop the first cup of sugar or sift an ounce of flour, they slip on their workshop aprons. A stencil pattern makes it easy for young painters to copy this design.

1. Trace and cut out the stencil pattern. Transfer the shaded areas of the pattern to the plastic. Cut out the design, using the craft knife. (**Note:** Child will need help with this step.)

2. Center the stencil on the right side of the apron bib, with the top of the house about 1" from the top of the apron. Tape the stencil in place.

3. Cover your work surface with newspaper. Pour a little paint onto the paper plate and paint the design green. Do not remove the stencil. Let the paint dry. If the design isn't dark enough, apply a second coat of paint. Remove the stencil when the paint is dry.

4. Glue on the buttons and the pom-poms as desired. Let the glue dry.

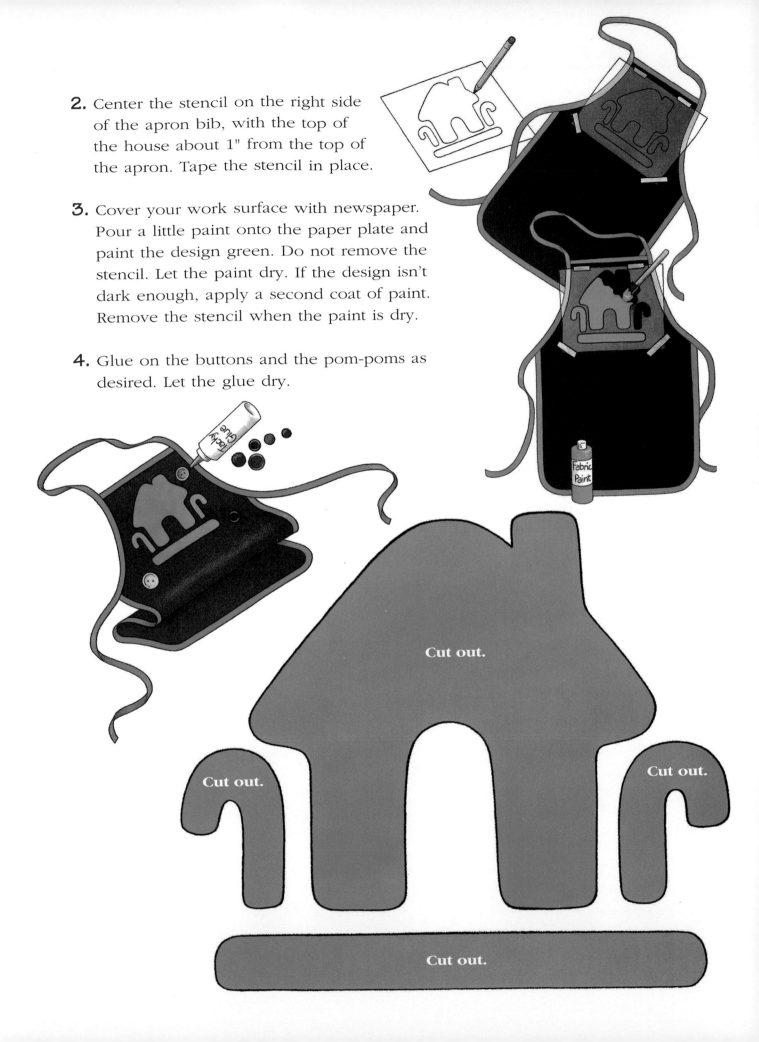

Cut out.

Cut out.

Cut out.

Cut out.

Button-Tree Top

Delight a child with a sweatshirt of buttons, easily glued on in the shape of a tree.

1. Place the sweatshirt faceup on a flat surface. Center 1 large green button 3½" below the neckband. Referring to the photograph at left and the illustration below, make additional rows of large green buttons approximately ¼" apart, adding 1 button to each new row and spacing the buttons in each row approximately 1" apart. Glue the large green buttons in place. Let the glue dry.

2. Center and glue 1 yellow star button above the top large green button and between the large green buttons of the third and fifth rows. Center and glue the red heart buttons between the large green buttons of the remaining rows. Let the glue dry.

3. For the tree trunk, center and glue the small green buttons in 2 rows ¼" below the last row of large green buttons, spacing the buttons in each row approximately ¼" apart. Let the glue dry.

**You will need
(for each sweatshirt):**
- Purchased white sweatshirt
- 21 (⅞") green buttons
- Fabric glue
- 7 (⁷⁄₁₆") yellow star buttons
- 9 (⁷⁄₁₆") red heart buttons
- 4 (⅝") green buttons

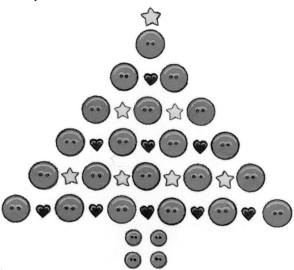

Reindeer Hats

These funny caps sport a pair of glove "antlers." Elmo gives them two "high fives."

You will need:

- 1 pair gloves
- Stuffing
- Pencil
- Cotton baseball cap
- Sewing needle
- Thread to match gloves

1. For the antlers, stuff the gloves to the desired fullness. Use the pencil to help work the stuffing into the fingers of the gloves if necessary.

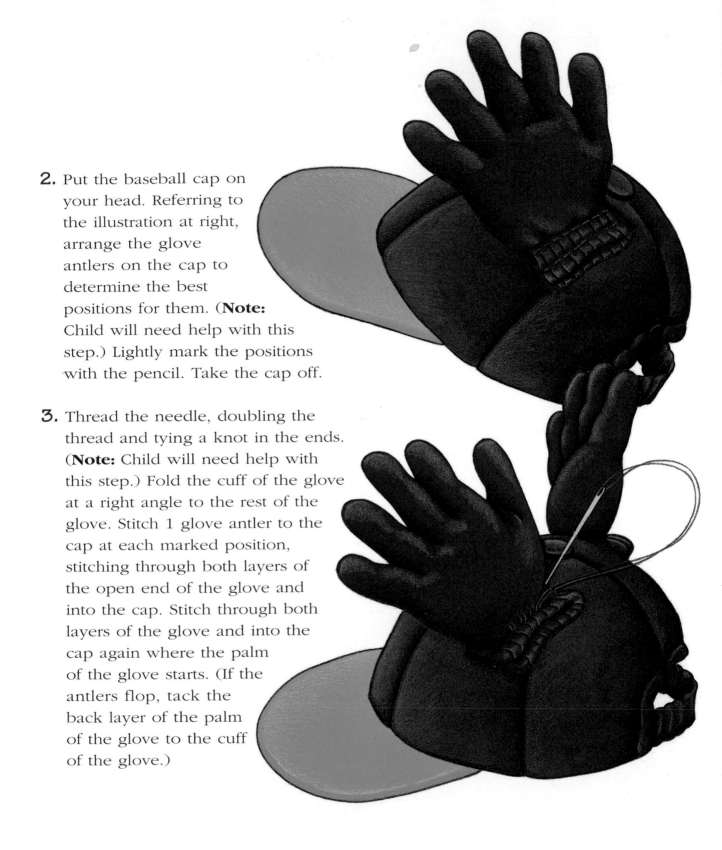

2. Put the baseball cap on your head. Referring to the illustration at right, arrange the glove antlers on the cap to determine the best positions for them. (**Note:** Child will need help with this step.) Lightly mark the positions with the pencil. Take the cap off.

3. Thread the needle, doubling the thread and tying a knot in the ends. (**Note:** Child will need help with this step.) Fold the cuff of the glove at a right angle to the rest of the glove. Stitch 1 glove antler to the cap at each marked position, stitching through both layers of the open end of the glove and into the cap. Stitch through both layers of the glove and into the cap again where the palm of the glove starts. (If the antlers flop, tack the back layer of the palm of the glove to the cuff of the glove.)

Wintertime Footgear

Bert and Ernie agree that sloshing through wintry slush is fun with boots decorated for the season.

1. Use the pencil to trace the stencil onto the paper side of the vinyl covering. Cut out, using the craft knife. (**Note:** Child will need help with this step.) Repeat to make as many stencils as desired.

2. Peel the paper backing off the stencils. Stick the stencils along the top edge of 1 boot, spacing evenly. Rub to make sure that all the edges adhere to the boot.

3. Squirt a blob of white paint onto the paper plate. Dip the paintbrush into the paint. Paint over the stencils, making sure the paint does not extend beyond the edges of the stencil. Let the paint dry.

4. Spray a light coat of varnish over the stenciled candy canes to help keep the paint from flaking off. (**Note:** Child will need help with this step.) Let the varnish dry.

You will need:
- Pattern below
- Peel-and-stick vinyl shelf covering
- Pencil
- Scissors
- Craft knife
- Purchased pair red rubber boots
- White brush-on acrylic paint
- Paper plate
- Paintbrush
- Spray varnish

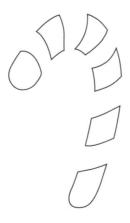

Index

Designers

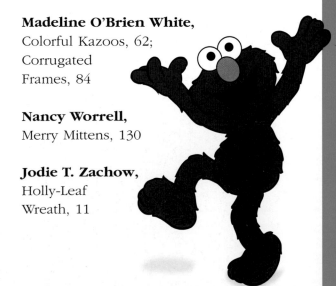